Bedtime Bible Story Book

Paradise Press, Inc.

Plantation, Florida

30962 - 895-1

By Shirley McCann Gee

Cover & Illustrations by
Eddie Roseboom

Printed in the U.S.A. All Rights Reserved.

Copyright © 1998
Paradise Press, Inc.
8551 Sunrise Blvd. #302
Plantation, FL 33322
954 • 476 • 5900

ISBN #1-57657-243-9

God Creates the Earth

Genesis 1:1-2:24

Once, long ago, there was no world at all. Then God decided to make the world. At first water covered the world and it was dark. But then God said, "Let there be light." And whatever God said happened. He called the light Day and the darkness Night. This was the first day.

On the second day God made the blue sky. He called the sky heaven.

The third day, God said the world needs land and water. He called the waters Seas and the dry land Earth. God also created grass, trees and beautiful flowers. God knew this was good work.

On the fourth day, God spoke again. He said, "Let the sun and moon and stars fill the sky." The sun was to shine in the day and the moon and stars would give light at night.

Then God created living creatures. The fish would swim in the seas and birds of every color and size would fly in the sky.

The fifth day passed and the world looked good.

It was on the sixth day that God put living creatures in the woods, on the plains, in the air and sea. He decided to make the first man. He took dust from the earth and made the body and then He breathed the breath of life into him. Man would have a soul. God called this man Adam. He was to rule over all other creatures. God made Adam a wife who was named Eve. At the end of the sixth day all was finished.

On the seventh day God rested.

1. *Name some of the things God created after he made the earth.*
2. *What was the name of the first man and woman on earth?*

Adam and Eve and the Serpent in the Garden

Genesis 2:8-3:7

God created a garden where Adam and Eve could live. For a while they lived there and they were very happy. They knew nothing about evil. God even walked and talked with them. They did what God told them to do. The garden was big and there were rivers running through it.

God planted two special trees in the garden. The first was called the tree of life. Whoever ate the fruit would live forever. Another tree was called the tree of knowledge of good and evil. God said, "You may eat the fruit of all the trees in the garden except from the tree of knowledge of good and evil. If you eat the fruit of that tree, you will die."

Now one of the animals in the garden was a serpent or snake. He was sneaky. One day the serpent asked Eve, "Will God let you eat the fruit of every tree in the garden?"

"We may eat from every tree except the tree of knowledge of good and evil. If we eat from it, we will die."

"That is not true! You will not die!" snorted the snake, "Eat it and you will be like God." Eve believed him and ate the fruit. She gave some to Adam and he ate it. At once Adam and Eve knew they had disobeyed God. Fear filled their hearts. For the first time they were afraid to meet with God.

1. *What did God tell Adam and Eve?*
2. *Why did Adam and Eve fear God and feel guilty after they ate the fruit?*

Adam and Eve Must Leave Their Home

Genesis 3:8-24

God walked in the beautiful garden but could not find Adam and Eve. They were hiding in the trees. God called to them. Adam said, "Lord, I heard you, but I was afraid. That is why I hid." God asked, "Why should you be afraid of me? Did you eat the forbidden fruit?" Adam said, "Eve gave me some of the fruit. I ate it." Eve told God, "The serpent tempted me so I ate the fruit."

God's heart was full of pain and sorrow because Adam and Eve had disobeyed him. They could no longer live in the garden. God sent them out into the world to make a home for themselves. God left an angel at the gate of the garden to make sure Adam and Eve could never go back in the garden.

God told the snake he would no longer have legs like other creatures. He would have to crawl over the earth. Then God told Eve, "Because you disobeyed me, you shall have pain and trouble for all of your days."

God felt Adam also had to be punished. He said to Adam, "Because you listened to your wife, you must suffer. You must work for everything." The fruits and vegetables would not be easy to grow. Weeds, thistles and thorns, would grow in the fields.

God sent them out of the Garden of Eden forever.

1. *How did God feel about Adam and Eve disobeying Him?*
2. *What happened to Adam and Eve when they left the garden?*

The Children, Cain and Abel

Genesis 4:1-16

Adam and Eve lived and worked out in the world. Soon God gave Adam and Eve the first child born in the world. Eve named the child Cain. Later Eve gave birth to a second son named Abel.

The two boys grew up and they worked just as their father had before them.

Cain was a farmer. Abel was a shepherd. Adam and Eve told their sons about God. They built altars to offer their gifts to God. Cain brought food from his field. Abel brought a lamb. God was pleased with Abel's gift, but He did not show favor to Cain.

Cain was very angry. God asked him, "Why are you so angry? If you do well, you will be accepted. If you do not, sin will take you. Do not let sin in your door. Master it!"

Cain and Abel went into the field and argued. Cain killed Abel. God asked Cain, "Where is your brother?" Cain answered, "I do not know. Am I my brother's keeper?"

God told Cain he would always live under a curse. Cain went away and built a town he named after his son, Enoch.

1. *Who was the first child born in the world?*
2. *What did God tell Cain?*

Noah and the Ark

Genesis 6:1-22

Many years went by and the earth was now full of people. But God was unhappy because most of the people were wicked. God decided to take all of the people off of earth.

God saw one good man named Noah. He went to Noah and told him to build a giant boat called an Ark. It would hold two of every animal. It looked like a three-story house. He built the boat on dry land. People laughed and laughed at Noah.

God told Noah he was going to send a flood, but God would save Noah and his family. Noah believed God so he did everything God told him.

1. *Why did God save Noah?*
2. *Who was allowed in the boat when the flood came?*

Noah and the Flood

Genesis 7:1-24

After Noah built the ark, God told Noah to take his whole family and go in the ark. God said Noah was a good man. God told Noah to take animals of every kind on the ark. He said, "I will send rain for forty days and forty nights. I will wipe from the face of the earth every living creature I have made."

Noah did what God told him to do. Noah and his wife and his three sons and the wives of his sons entered the ark with all of the animals. Noah was 600 years old when the rain started.

The rain fell as God said it would. The water covered the ground and continued to rain. The ark rose high above the earth. The water rose above the mountains by more than twenty feet. Every living thing on the earth died. Only Noah and those on the ark lived. The water stayed on the earth for 150 days.

1. *Who was allowed on the ark?*
2. *How long did it rain?*

The Promise and the Rainbow

Genesis 8:1-9:17

God sent the wind to blow on the earth. Finally one day Noah sent a dove out of the ark. When the dove returned with an olive leaf in her mouth, Noah knew the earth was dry.

God spoke to Noah. He told Noah to go forth from the ark. Noah took his family and the animals off of the ark and he built an altar. He gave gifts to God for saving his family. God was pleased.

God made a promise. "I sign the covenant between you and Me and every living creature with you. I will never destroy the earth again. There will always be seasons and day and night." To remind everyone of his promise God created the rainbow in the sky.

1. *How did Noah show he was grateful to God for saving him and his family?*
2. *What is the sign in the sky that God will keep his promise?*

The Tower of Babel

Genesis 11:1-9

The earth had people again after Noah's sons had children and those children had children. These people all moved to the valley called Mesopotamia. They decided to build a city with a tower so high it would reach the sky. The city was called Babel which means "confusion." It was later called Babylon.

The people were excited about building the tower. They made bricks and mortar. They worked hard.

But God was not pleased. He knew the people were beginning to think more about "things" and themselves than about what God had given them. He was afraid life would become wicked again as it had been before the flood. God did not want all of the people living in one place.

Something strange began to happen. Until this time all people spoke one language. Neighbors began speaking different languages. Workers could not understand each other. Some of the people who spoke the same language left the town. They went to live in other parts of the world.

1. *What did God do to the people of Babel?*
2. *Why did the people move away?*

Abram Follows God

Genesis 12:1-9

Near Babel was another city named Haran. God spoke to a man there named Abram. Abram was a good man. God told Abram, "I will make you into a great nation and I will bless you; I will make your name great. I will curse whoever curses you. All of the people on earth will be blessed through you."

Abram took his wife, Sarai, and his nephew, Lot, and his family and all of the things they owned. They left Haran and traveled through the land to Canaan. God appeared again and said, "To you and all those after you I will give this land." Abram built an altar and worshiped God. God appeared to him.

From there Abram went on toward the hills east of Bethel and pitched his tent. He built another altar to God.

1. Why did God pick Abram to be blessed?
2. What did Abram do to show his thanks to God?

Abram and Lot

Genesis 13

When Abram went to Canaan, his nephew, Lot, went with him. Abram became a very rich man. He owned flocks of sheep, gold and silver. Lot was successful, too.

He had servants, sheep and cattle. People followed them wherever they pitched their tents.

Trouble arose between the servants of Abram and Lot. They fought over land.

Abram told Lot, "Let there be no trouble between you and me for we are family."

He knew there was plenty of room for all. Abram let Lot choose the land he wanted.

Lot chose the rich land where the Jordan river flows. It was close to the cities of Sodom and Gomorrah. It was some of the best land there was.

Abram moved his tents to Hebron. There he built an altar to God.

1. *Who was Lot?*
2. *How did Abram show he was generous?*

God's Promise to Abram

Genesis 15:1-18

After Abram settled in Hebron God came to him and said, "Do not fear. Your reward shall be great." But Abram was worried for he had no children. He said, "God, I am an old man. Who will get this reward?" God said, "Look toward heaven and count the stars. That is how big your family will be." Abram was confused but he believed God.

God then made a covenant with Abram just as he had with Noah. A covenant is a promise between two people. Each one agrees to do something. God promised to give Abram a son, a people and a land. Abram promised to serve God faithfully.

1. *What was the best reward God gave Abram?*
2. *What is a covenant?*

Abram Walks with God

Genesis 17

Abram was now a very old man. He was 99 years old. God came to him again. He said, "Abram, I am now ready to fulfill my covenant to you. You and your wife shall have a child and that child shall have children and those children many children. You will be the father of a multitude."

Because Abram would be the first of many generations, God told Abram he would now be called Abraham which means "father of a multitude." His wife Sarai would be called Sarah which means "princess."

1. *What was the covenant God gave Abraham?*
2. *What does the new name Abraham mean?*

Sarah Has Doubt

Genesis 18:1-15

O n another day Abraham was sitting in the shade of an oak tree near his tent. He saw God and two angels standing near by. Abraham rushed in to Sarah, his wife, and told her to make a good lunch.

He then rushed out to greet the three. God asked, "Where is your wife, Abraham? She will soon have a child." Sarah was very old. She was in the tent and heard what God had said. "Why does she laugh?" God remarked. "Is anything too hard for me? In the spring Sarah will have a child!"

1. *What was Sarah doing in the tent?*
2. *Why did Sarah laugh?*

Lot Leaves Sodom

Genesis 19:1-24

The angels left God and Abraham and went to find Lot in Sodom. They found him. Sodom had become a sinful town. There were few good people in the town. God did not want the towns to become as they were before the flood.

The angels warned Lot to leave immediately. Lot did not understand why he should leave. The angels grabbed his hand. They also took the hands of his daughters and his wife. They warned Lot and his family to run for the hills and not look back.

God poured fire on Sodom that looked as thick as rain. Smoke was all over the valley. Lot's wife looked back at the city. She then turned into a pillar of salt. The rest of the family kept running. They were safe.

1. Why did God destroy Sodom?
2. Why do you think Lot's wife looked back? What happened to her?

Abraham and His Sons

Genesis 21:1-14

Abraham soon moved his camp closer to the sea. As had been promised, Sarah gave birth to a baby boy. Abraham was now 100 years old. They named the child Isaac as the angel had told them to. Isaac means "laughing." There was a great feast in his honor.

There were now two boys in Abraham's tent. Ishmael was the son of Hagar, a servant to Sarah and Abraham. Ishmael did not treat Isaac kindly. This made Sarah mad. She told Abraham to send Ishmael and Hagar away.

Abraham was sad for Ishmael was also his son. But God told Abraham not to worry. God promised to take care of Ishmael. He said Ishmael and Isaac would both be the father of a great family.

The next morning Abraham sent Ishmael and Hagar away.

1. *How did Abraham and Sarah feel when Isaac was born?*
2. *Why did Abraham send Ishmael and Hagar away?*

Hagar and Ishmael Sent Away

Genesis 21:14-20

Early one morning Abraham took some food and a pouch of water to Hagar. He told her to go and take Ishmael away. She wandered around in the desert.

When the water was all gone, she put Ishmael under a bush. She thought her son was going to die. She sat down nearby and began to cry.

Ishmael also began to cry and God heard him. The angel of God called to Hagar and told her not to be afraid. God would take care of Ishmael. "Take the boy by the hand and lead him," the angel said. God promised to make him into a great nation.

When Hagar opened her eyes she saw a well of water. She was happy and she gave the boy a drink.

God kept his promise. He watched the boy grow up. Ishmael lived in the desert and became an archer.

1. *Why was Hagar afraid for her son?*
2. *Who spoke to her and what was the promise?*

Abraham Offers Isaac

Genesis 22:1-19

God would test Abraham. He said to him, "Abraham, take your son, Isaac, whom you love, and go to Moriah. Sacrifice him there as a burnt offering on one of the mountains."

The next day Abraham got up early and saddled his donkey. He cut wood for an offering. He took Isaac and two servants and went to the place God had told him about. It took three days to travel there.

Abraham left the donkey with the servants and took the boy. He told the servants he was going to worship. He handed the wood to his son. He took the fire and the knife.

Isaac was confused. As they walked he said, "Father, we have fire and wood, but we do not have a lamb for the offering." Abraham answered, "God will send us a lamb."

They reached the place where God had told him to go. Abraham built an altar. He arranged the wood on it. He took Isaac and bound him and laid him on the altar. He raised his knife. But God told Abraham to put the knife down. Abraham proved to God that he feared Him and loved Him.

Abraham saw a ram caught in some bushes. He took the ram and used it as the burnt offering sacrifice.

God called to Abraham, "Because you have done this, I will bless you and your son and all of his future children. Through these children all nations on earth will be blessed because you have obeyed me."

Abraham and Isaac and the servants returned to their home.

1. *What sacrifice did God ask Abraham to make?*
2. *What promise did God make to Abraham?*

A Wife for Isaac

Genesis 24:1-27

Isaac grew up and was old enough to be married. Abraham knew he needed to find a wife for Isaac. Abraham was getting old. He sent for a servant to go back to his homeland.

Abraham wanted Isaac to marry a woman from his own family. It was important that his wife worship God as Isaac did.

The servant took camels and gifts. He traveled to the city of Nahor and then stopped at the well. He prayed he would find a good wife for Isaac. He looked up and saw a beautiful young woman. He asked if she would give him a drink.

"You may have water," she said, " and your camels need water, too."

"What is your name?" the servant asked.

"I am Rebekah. Come stay at our house." The servant found that Rebekah was the daughter of Bethuel, a brother to Abraham.

The servant gave Rebekah gold earrings and bracelets as gifts. He told her he was from Abraham's house. He thanked God and said a prayer.

1. *Why was it important to find a wife in Abraham's homeland?*
2. *Who was Rebekah's father?*

Esau and Jacob

Genesis 25:21-34

Isaac and Rebekah married when Isaac was forty. Rebekah could not have children. Isaac prayed to God for children. God answered the prayer by giving Isaac and Rebekah twin boys when Isaac was sixty. Rebekah named the boys Esau and Jacob.

Esau was the first born son. In those times that meant that he would get twice as much as Jacob when Isaac died. This was called a birthright.

The boys grew up. Isaac loved Esau and Rebekah loved Jacob. Esau was a hunter and loved wild meat. Jacob was a quiet man.

Once when Jacob was cooking some stew, Esau returned from a day in the wild very hungry. "I'm so hungry!" said Esau, "Let me have some of that stew." Jacob said, "Sell me your birthright for the stew." Esau agreed because he was so hungry and he did not cherish his birthright.

Jacob took advantage of Esau. That was not right. But Esau was foolish to sell his birthright. This, too, was wrong.

1. *Who were the sons of Isaac and Rebekah?*
2. *What is a birthright?*

Isaac Blesses Jacob

Genesis 27:1-36

Isaac was now old and blind. He knew he would die soon. He wanted to give his blessing to Esau. He called to Esau and said, "Take your bow and arrow, go into the woods, and kill some game. Bring me the delicious meat after you cook it. After I have eaten I will give you my blessing." Esau hurried to the woods. Now he wished he had not sold his birthright.

Rebekah heard the conversation between father and son. She quickly cooked some meat that she knew Isaac liked. She gave it to Jacob. "Take this to your father and pretend you are Esau. He is blind and will not know. Then you will get the blessing."

At first Jacob was afraid his father would recognize him and put a curse on him. Jacob did what his mother told him. Isaac did not recognize Jacob. Isaac thought he was blessing Esau.

When Esau returned, Isaac realized that he had blessed the wrong son. Esau wept for he had lost the blessing and his birthright.

1. *Why did Rebekah cook a special meal for Isaac?*
2. *By playing a trick on his father, what did Jacob gain?*

Jacob's Dream

Genesis 27:41-28:22

Rebekah heard Esau say that he wanted to kill Jacob for all that he had done. She called for Jacob. She told him to go immediately to visit her brother Laban. Jacob was to stay with Laban until Esau's anger had passed.

Jacob went alone into the desert. He had a staff or walking stick. He stopped at a certain place and he picked up a stone to use as his pillow. He placed his head on the stone and quickly fell asleep.

While he was asleep he had a dream. He dreamed there was a stairway between earth and heaven. Angels were walking up and down the stairs. At the top of the stairs stood the Lord. He said, "I am the Lord God of your father Abraham and the God of Isaac. I will give you and your descendants the land upon which you are lying All peoples on the earth will be blessed through you and your offspring."

When Jacob awoke from his sleep, he knew God was with him. He said, "The Lord is in this place and I did not know it. This place is the house of God and the gate of heaven." Jacob named the place Bethel because in his language that meant The House of God.

Jacob took the stone he had used as a pillow. He poured oil on it as an offering to God. Jacob said, " If God will stay with me as promised and give me the items He promised, I will worship God and return to him one-tenth of what I have as an offering."

1. *What was Jacob's dream?*
2. *Why did Jacob name the place Bethel?*

Jacob's Wives

Genesis 29:1-30:24

Jacob continued on his journey to find Laban, his uncle. He came to the city of Haran. There he found the same well where the servant had found his mother, Rebekah. A young woman was watering her sheep. This was Rachel, daughter of Laban. He fell in love with Rachel at the well.

Jacob went to Laban. Jacob told him he would work for him for seven years if he could marry Rachel. Laban agreed.

Seven years passed. The day of the wedding the bride wore a thick veil. When the wedding was over and Jacob lifted the veil he realized he had married Leah, Rachel's older sister. He felt he had been cheated by Laban. Laban told Jacob that it was the custom for the oldest to marry first. It would be unfair for Rachel to marry before Leah.

Laban promised that if Jacob worked seven more years, Rachel could be his bride. He loved Rachel so much that he agreed to seven more years of work. It was not uncommon for men to have more than one wife. Finally after seven more years, Jacob married Rachel.

While Jacob was living in Haran, eleven sons were born to him. The youngest son was Joseph, the only child belonging to his beloved wife Rachel. Jacob loved Joseph best.

1. *How did Laban cheat Jacob?*
2. *Why did Jacob work another seven years for Laban?*

Jacob Leaves for Home

Genesis 31:17-32:22

Jacob became rich while he lived with Laban. He worked hard and was very careful and wise. It was time for him to return to Canaan. Jacob packed up his large family. He gathered his herd of animals and started his journey. He did not tell Laban he was leaving.

Laban's sons told Laban about Jacob's plans. Laban was sad. He wanted Jacob and his family to stay near him. He liked the way Jacob handled his business. Laban caught up with Jacob in the hills. There they promised not to harm each other. Both men knew that God was watching them.

Jacob set up a stone for a pillar and the other men gathered stones in a heap. Laban called this heap Mizpah, which means "a watchtower." Laban said to Jacob, "May God watch over us while we are absent from one another." Jacob agreed. Both packed their supplies and left for their separate homes.

1. *Why did Laban want Jacob to stay?*
2. *What was the promise (covenant) Laban made to Jacob?*

Wrestling with God and Reuniting with a Brother

Genesis 32:24-33:18

Jacob was alone when a man grabbed him. The two wrestled until dawn when Jacob realized the man was an angel of God. The angel said, "Let me go for it is almost day." Jacob replied, "I am Jacob and I will not let you go until you have blessed me." The angel said, "You have wrestled with God and men. You have won. Your name shall no longer be Jacob, but Israel." From that time forward all of people from that area, Jacob's descendants, were called Israelites.

Jacob continued toward home. Soon he saw his brother Esau coming toward him. He was afraid to meet his brother after all of this time. He did not know how Esau felt about him. Esau ran to Jacob and threw his arms around him. All was forgiven. Jacob, or Israel, took his family and lived in the land of Canaan.

1. *What new name did the angel give Jacob?*
2. *What happened when Esau and Jacob met after years apart?*

Joseph, a Dreamer

Genesis 35:16-37:11

All was well with Jacob and his family in Canaan. Rachel gave Jacob another child. But when the time came for the child to be born, Rachel died. Jacob mourned. He named the twelfth son Benjamin.

Jacob turned his love to his favorite son, Joseph. When Jacob made a wonderful coat of many colors for Joseph, the older brothers showed their jealousy and hatred for their brother.

Joseph always did as he was told. One day he told his father when he saw four of his brothers do wrong. The brothers disliked Joseph even more.

One night seventeen-year-old Joseph said to his brothers, "Listen to the dreams I have had." When Joseph told them the dreams, his brothers knew their meaning. Some day all of them would bow down to Joseph. The brothers now hated Joseph because of his dreams.

1. What special gift did Jacob give Joseph?
2. Why were his brothers jealous of Joseph?

Joseph Is Sold as a Slave

Genesis 37:12-35

While the sons of Jacob were tending flocks, Jacob worried over their safety. He decided to send Joseph to find out if they were safe. The brothers saw his bright colored coat. "Here comes that dreamer!" said one. "Let's kill him and pretend an animal did it," said another, "then we'll see what comes of his dreams."

Reuben, the oldest brother, convinced the other brothers to throw him in a pit to die. They removed his beautiful coat and threw him in the dry pit. Reuben planned to rescue Joseph.

Reuben was away when a caravan of Ishmaelites came. The brothers sold Joseph for twenty silver pieces. The Ishmaelites took Joseph to Egypt.

The sons all knew they had to tell their father what happened to Joseph. They decided to lie. They killed an animal, covered Joseph's coat with blood and gave it to Jacob when they returned home. The old man mourned bitterly and could not be comforted, but the brothers would not tell their father what they had done.

Meanwhile, Joseph was taken to Egypt and sold to Potiphar, one of the Pharaoh's officials.

1. *What did Reuben tell the brothers to do with Joseph?*
2. *Why did they stain Joseph's coat with animal blood?*

Joseph the Slave

Genesis 39:1-40:23

While in Egypt Joseph lived as a slave in the house of his Egyptian master, Potiphar, an officer in the army of the Pharaoh. Joseph was well-liked by Potiphar. He was in charge of all of the servants in the house. At first Potiphar's wife also liked Joseph, but she wanted him to do wrong for her and he refused. She lied to her husband about Joseph. Potiphar believed his wife. He put Joseph in prison.

But even in prison Joseph knew God was with him. He was happy and cheerful. The jailer knew he was special so he put him in charge of the prison.

Some time later the butler and the baker of the Pharaoh were both sent to prison. They had dreams which frightened them. It was common in those days for God to talk to people in dreams. The two did not understand their dreams. Joseph offered to listen and tell them what the dreams meant.

He decided the butler would be turned free. The butler was freed from prison. Joseph asked the butler to tell the king that Joseph was in prison. The baker's dream was sad. Joseph told him he would be hanged for his crime. The dreams came true just as Joseph had told the men they would.

1. *Why was Joseph put in prison?*
2. *How did Joseph know what the other prisoner's dreams meant?*

Pharaoh's Dreams

Genesis 4:23-41:43

It was two years before the butler thought to tell the Pharaoh about Joseph and the dreams. The butler did not remember until the Pharaoh had dreams himself. He was trying to find out the meaning of his own dreams. The magicians did not know their meaning. No one knew. The butler told of his experience in jail. He suggested the Pharaoh call on Joseph.

The Pharaoh sent for Joseph. "Can you tell me the meaning of my dreams?" asked the Pharaoh. "The power is not with me," Joseph stated, " but God will give you the answers."

The Pharaoh told Joseph about the two dreams. Joseph told the Pharaoh the two dreams meant the same thing. There would be good crops in Egypt for seven years. Then there will be seven years with no food. Food should be saved during the first seven years to use when there will be no crops.

"The Pharaoh should find a wise man to plan for the famine," said Joseph. The Pharaoh answered, "Since God has made all of this known to you, you shall be in charge."

The Pharaoh put his own ring on Joseph's finger. He dressed him in fine clothes and put a gold chain around his neck. Joseph was in charge of all of the land. God had not forgotten Joseph.

1. *Why did the butler remember to tell the Pharaoh about Joseph?*
2. *What did Joseph tell the Pharaoh he should do about the dreams?*

Joseph Sees His Brothers

Genesis 41:46-42:24

Joseph was thirty years old when he started working for the Pharaoh. He traveled all through Egypt. For the next seven years there was plenty of food. Joseph saw that much of it was saved. During this time Joseph married and had two sons.

After seven years the famine began just as Joseph said it would. The Pharaoh's people had plenty of food. However, other parts of the world had no food. They went to the Pharaoh for food. The Pharaoh told anyone who came to him to go to Joseph.

Joseph sold food to everyone who came looking for it. In Canaan Jacob heard that there was food in Egypt. He sent his sons to find food. They came to the room and bowed down to him. Joseph recognized his brothers. The brothers did not know who Joseph was.

Joseph thought they came as spies. They all argued. The brothers were locked up. Joseph finally called for them and said, "One of you stay here. Go bring your youngest brother. Then I will know you are not spies." Simeon was chosen to stay. Reuben said to his brothers, "This has happened because of what you did to Joseph." Joseph overheard them. He now knew his brothers were sorry for what they had done. He left the room and wept.

1. *Why did Joseph store up food?*
2. *Why did Joseph weep?*

Joseph's Brothers Return

Genesis 42:25-43:15

Joseph did not want his brothers to pay for the food. Joseph had their money packed in the sacks of food. When the brothers returned home they found the money. They were frightened. Jacob was upset. He had lost Joseph and Simeon and now they wanted to take Benjamin away.

With such a large family the food did not last long. More was needed. "We cannot go unless we take Benjamin," said the brothers.

Jacob finally agreed. "Take some spices and myrrh. Take double the amount of silver, for you must return the silver that was left in the sacks by mistake. May God grant you mercy," he wept.

The brothers returned once again to Egypt. They took Benjamin with them. Soon they bowed once again before Joseph.

1. *Why was Joseph hard on his brothers?*
2. *Why did the brothers go back to Egypt?*

Joseph Makes Himself Known

Genesis 43-16-45:16

When Joseph saw his little brother, Benjamin, he told the servants, "Take these men to my house for a feast." The brothers were afraid to go to Joseph's house. "We have returned the money," they cried out. "Don't be afraid. Your God gave you that money," said a servant. Simeon was brought in to join the brothers. Joseph entered and all bowed to him.

Joseph started questioning the group, "How is your father? Is he alive?" He saw Benjamin, his mother's son. He looked at him with love, but he rushed to a private room to weep.

After the men had eaten the feast, Joseph had the servants fill the sacks with as much food as they would hold. He then told them to leave the silver in the sacks. Joseph's silver cup was placed in Benjamin's bag.

After the brothers were on the road Joseph sent his steward to check the bags and find the one which held his cup. The brothers were afraid and said they did not take anything. All returned to Egypt. Joseph said he would make a slave of the brother who took his cup. He knew this was Benjamin, the brother Joseph loved.

Judah, one of Jacob's sons spoke, "Our father is very old. If Benjamin does not return, his father will no doubt die."

Joseph could not keep his secret any longer. "I am Joseph, your brother! You sold me into slavery, but God wanted this." He and Benjamin hugged and talked.

1. *Why did Jacob send extra gifts when his son returned for more food?*
2. *Why did Joseph give Benjamin more than the others?*

Jacob Goes to Egypt

Genesis 45:25-49:33

The brothers went out of Egypt to the land of Canaan. They told Jacob, their father, that Joseph was still alive. He was so surprised he did not believe them at first. They showed him the carts and other things Joseph had sent with them. And Jacob, now called Israel, said "I am convinced. I will go to see him before I die."

Israel set out with all of his family for Egypt. He made sacrifices to God. God told him, "Do not be afraid to go to Egypt. Your family will become a great nation there."

Israel saw Joseph and his sons. Israel told Joseph, "Now that I have seen you and your sons I can die in peace." He blessed both sons.

Israel then gathered all of his sons and told them what was to happen. He blessed his sons. He told them of their future. They would be called the twelve tribes of Israel. Israel told his sons to take him back to Canaan and bury him with his father, Isaac, and grandfather, Abraham. When Israel had finished giving his instructions about the future and about his burial, he breathed his last breath.

1. *Why did Jacob want to go to Egypt?*
2. *Where did Jacob want to be buried?*

The Death of Joseph

Genesis 50:15-26

When Joseph's father died his brothers were worried. "What if Joseph holds a grudge against us for all of the things we have done to him?" The brothers sent Joseph a message explaining that his father had asked Joseph to forgive the brothers their sins.

Joseph was upset at the message. He told his brothers, "Don't be afraid. I will provide for you and your children."

Joseph lived in Egypt with his father's family for the rest of his life. Joseph lived 110 years. When he was about to die, he told his brothers that God would come to their aid. God had promised to take them out of this land to the land that was promised. When he died his body was placed in a coffin. Someday Joseph's coffin would be taken back to their own land.

1. *Why were Joseph's brothers afraid when their father died?*
2. *What did Joseph remind them would happen?*

Moses in the Basket

Exodus 1:1-2:10

Years later there was a new ruler who did not remember Joseph. Pharaoh was afraid Israel would become more powerful than Egypt. The Israelites were forced into slavery. They built the cities for Pharaoh, and they worked his crops. Pharaoh decided to protect Egypt. He gave this order, "Every boy that is born must be thrown in the Nile, but every girl may live."

A baby boy was born. For three months his mother hid him from the soldiers. When the baby was too old to hide, she gathered bulrushes that grew along the river. She wove these into a basket. She made a strong bed in the bottom. It was hard, but she put the baby in the basket and placed it in the river. The basket floated among the reeds.

Pharaoh's daughter came to the river with other women. She found the basket and knew it must be an Israelite child. She decided to keep the baby and call him Moses.

1. *Why did Pharaoh want to kill Israelite boys?*
2. *How was Moses saved and who saved him?*

Moses Becomes a Shepherd

Exodus 2:11-25

Although Moses grew up in the palace of Pharaoh among the Egyptians, he loved his own people. The Egyptians worshiped idols and animals while the Israelites worshiped God.

Moses tried to help his people but they were unsure of him because of his relationship with Pharaoh. Pharaoh became unhappy with him because he tried to help the Israelites. Moses ran away from Egypt to Midian.

After the long journey, he sat by a well to rest. Young women were trying to water their flocks. Some rough shepherds tried to drive them away. Moses helped the women. The women were all the daughters of Jethro. Jethro invited Moses to stay in his home. Moses later married Jethro's daughter, Zipporah.

Moses lived in Egypt forty years. Now he was herding another man's flock. He said, "I have become a stranger in a foreign land."

Changes were taking place in Egypt. The old Pharaoh died. The Israelites were more miserable. Their hearts were heavy. They prayed to God. God heard the prayers, and he remembered His covenant with Abraham, Isaac and Jacob.

1. *Why did Moses run away from Egypt?*
2. *Why did God make Moses a shepherd?*

The Burning Bush

Exodus 3:1-10

Moses was tending the flock of Jethro, his father-in-law. He led the flock to one side of the desert near the mountain of God. An angel of the Lord appeared to him in the flame of a fire from within a bush. Moses was alarmed that the bush was on fire but did not burn up.

Moses thought, "I will go over and see this strange sight." God called to him, "Moses! Moses!" Moses answered, "Here I am." God told Moses to take off his sandals for he was standing on holy ground. "I am the God of Abraham, Isaac and Jacob." Moses hid his face because he was afraid to look at God.

"I have seen the misery of your people in Egypt. I have heard them cry. I have come down to rescue them from the Egyptians. I am sending you to Pharaoh to bring the Israelites out of Egypt."

1. What was strange about the burning bush?
2. Where did God send Moses?

Moses Returns to Egypt

Exodus 3:11-4:31

Moses was amazed that God wanted him to bring the Israelites out of Egypt. God wanted the Israelites to go to Canaan, a place that flows with milk and honey. Moses did not think he could do what God asked. Moses questioned, "Suppose the Israelites want to know who is sending me. What shall I tell them?" God answered, "Say to the Israelites, 'The God of your fathers has sent me to you.' If they ask my name, answer I AM who I am. I AM sent me to you.'"

Still concerned, Moses asked, "What if they still don't believe me?" God told Moses to throw down his shepherd's staff. When Moses did, the staff became a snake. "There will be other signs to you," said God.

God sent Moses' brother, Aaron, to go with Moses to Goshen. The two told the Israelite leaders what God had told them. The leaders believed. When they heard the Lord was concerned about them, they bowed down and prayed.

1. *What did Moses tell God to do?*
2. *What was a sign that Moses was from God?*

Moses and Aaron Go to Pharaoh

Exodus 5:1-7:13

One day Moses and Aaron went to see the Pharaoh The two told Pharaoh, "This is what our Lord, the God of Israel, says: 'Let my people go so they may worship in the wilderness.'" Pharaoh asked why Moses and Aaron would take the people away from their work. Pharaoh became very angry. He said the people were lazy. He made the Israelites suffer and work even more.

Moses prayed to God. He asked God why He was allowing Pharaoh to place more trouble on these people. God told him to go to Pharaoh and show him the signs. So Moses and Aaron returned. Aaron threw down the staff, and it became a snake. Pharaoh called for his magicians. The magicians did the same. Their staffs turned to snakes. But Aaron's staff swallowed the staffs of the magicians.

1. *Why did Pharaoh give the Israelites more work?*
2. *What happened when Aaron threw down his staff?*

The Plagues of Blood and Frogs

Exodus 7:14-8:15

The next morning God sent Moses and Aaron to Pharaoh again. They met on the bank of the Nile river. Because God had sent them, Moses and Aaron were not afraid. God had told them Pharaoh would have a hard heart.

Aaron took the staff with him. Moses told him to hit the water with it. When Aaron struck the river with the staff, the river turned to blood. The fish died, and the smell was terrible.

There was no water to drink.

Seven days later God sent Moses and Aaron back to Pharaoh. "God says, 'Let my people go,'" said Moses. The Pharaoh refused. Aaron held the staff over the river. Frogs covered Egypt. Frogs were found in ovens, houses, and beds.

Pharaoh finally called to Moses and Aaron. He told them to pray to their Lord to take away the frogs from Egypt, and he would let the Israelites go. Moses asked and the Lord let all of the frogs die in one day. Pharaoh tricked Moses and Aaron. He did not let the people go.

1. *Why did God make the river turn to blood?*
2. *How did Pharaoh break his promise?*

More Plagues in Egypt

Exodus 8:16-10:29

Pharaoh would not let God's people go. Aaron used the staff again. When he hit the ground with the staff, all of the dust turned into fleas. Fleas bit the people and the animals. Still Pharaoh would not listen.

Moses once again asked Pharaoh to free the Israelites. Once again he refused. God sent flies. Dense swarms of flies covered the palace of the Pharaoh both inside and out. All of the land in Egypt was ruined by flies. Pharaoh told Moses to pray to God to let the flies go away, and he would let the people go. Again he broke his promise.

This time a terrible disease came to all of the animals in Egypt. The animals had sores over all of their bodies. But Pharaoh still would not let the people go. Then hail fell on Egypt. The hail killed everything, but Pharaoh still did not fear the Lord. Next grasshoppers were sent. The grasshoppers ate everything that was left.

Finally, Egypt was dark for three days. Pharaoh said go worship, but leave your animals. Moses refused to go without the animals. Animals were needed for sacrifices. Pharaoh was mad. He told Moses to get out of his sight. He never wanted to see Moses again. "You are right," said Moses, "I will never see you again."

1. *What different plagues were sent to Egypt?*
2. *Why did these terrible things happen?*

The Passover

Exodus 12:1-30

G od said to Moses, "It is now a new year for all of my people. Every family should find a good lamb. They should kill the lamb. The blood should be placed on the door frame. There must be blood on every door. Then roast the lamb. Every family should have a feast. Eat it, but be ready to travel quickly. It is my Passover."

God continued, "Near midnight I will pass through Egypt. The oldest son in every family will die, including the son of Pharaoh. There will be more crying in Egypt then has ever been heard. If there is blood on the door, I will pass you by. That will be the way you will know the difference between Egypt and Israel. Keep this day as a feast each year."

1. *What were the Israelites to place on the frame of the door?*
2. *What would the "passover" prevent from happening?*

The Exodus

12:31-14:9

When the Pharaoh found his son dead he called to Moses and Aaron. "Leave this land, you and all the Israelites! Leave and leave quickly!"

There now were over six hundred thousand men plus their wives and children. They took their flocks and herds. They took the bread which did not yet have yeast. When they stopped for the night, the women baked cakes of unleavened bread.

God said, "Celebrate the day you have left Egypt." From that time on the Israelites celebrated one week every year as the Feast of Unleavened Bread.

The Israelites took the coffin of Joseph with them when they left Egypt. As promised they took the body and buried it at Canaan.

God was the leader of the Israelites. During the day they followed a great cloud. At night there was a pillar of fire. God was always with them. Pharaoh was sorry he let them go. He had no slaves to do his work. With his army Pharaoh followed the Israelites.

1. *What was the important item left out of the bread?*
2. *What were the signs God gave the Israelites that He was leading them?*

The Red Sea

Exodus 14:10-31

The Israelites were trapped between the army of the Pharaoh and the Red Sea. The Israelites were afraid. They told Moses they were better off serving Pharaoh than dying in the desert. Moses answered the people, "Do not be afraid. The Lord will help you."

Then the Lord told Moses to raise his staff over the sea. Moses did what the Lord told him. The water divided so the Israelites could go through to dry ground. There was a wall of water on the right and a wall of water on the left.

Pharaoh and the Egyptian army followed the Israelites. By this time the Israelites were on dry ground. God told Moses to once again raise his staff over the water. Once again Moses did as the Lord told him. The sea returned. It covered the soldiers, their horses, and their chariots. The Lord saved the Israelites from the Egyptians. The people feared the Lord and put their trust in Him and Moses.

1. *What happened when Moses raised his staff over the Red Sea?*
2. *What happened to the Egyptian army?*

Water for Thirsty Israelites

Exodus 15:22-27

The Israelites celebrated after they were delivered from the Egyptian Army. They soon began their march across the wilderness. This land was more like a desert.

They came to a place called Marah which means "bitter." Everyone was thirsty. The people were thirsty. The animals were thirsty. Moses was thirsty. Everyone was hot and tired. At Marah the Israelites found a spring of water, but when they tasted the water it was bitter. They could not drink it.

Moses asked God for help. Growing near the spring was a tree. God told Moses to cut down the tree and throw it in the water. This made the water fresh. It tasted sweet and cool.

God was still trying to get the people to trust him. He told them, "If you will listen to the voice of God, if you will do what is right, if you will trust Me, I will be with you and heal you."

The Israelites soon moved on until they found a place with palm trees and twelve wells of water. The people pitched their tents and drank from the wells.

1. *How did the water taste?*
2. *What was God trying to teach the Israelites?*

Food from God

Exodus 16

The Israelites received signs from God to move once again. They walked to an area called the Desert of Sin. Once again the people began to whine. There was no food. Perhaps they should have stayed in Egypt. The Israelites had already forgotten how awful it was in Egypt.

Moses was upset. He went to God again, and again God told Moses he would take care of the people. He would not let them die of hunger. God would send bread from heaven in the morning and meat at night. Each day there was white frost on the ground. "What is it?" said the people. They called it manna meaning "what is this?". They made cakes from the manna. Each evening quail flew into the camp. They ate the quail.

Moses told the people there would be manna every day. They were to gather only what they needed for that day. On the sixth day they were to gather enough for two days so they would not have to work on the Sabbath. They also were not to gather more than they needed to eat each day.

Most of the people did what Moses told them. Some people gathered too much, but the bread spoiled. Some people did not gather extra on the sixth day. There was no manna on the ground on the Sabbath.

God sent enough manna to the Israelites every morning for all of the years until they reached the border of Canaan.

1. *Where did the manna come from?*
2. *What were the Israelites to do on the sixth day?*

The Ten Commandments

Exodus 19:1-24:18

For three months the Israelites traveled until they entered the Desert of Sinai where they camped near a mountain. God spoke to Moses from the mountain, "This is a holy place. In three days the people will see me on the mountain top."

In three days all were waiting for God. There was smoke and fire in a cloud. The mountain shook. Moses spoke to God. The people heard thunder. They were afraid, and they thought they would die. Moses told the people, "Do not be afraid when God speaks. He wants to teach you that he is a Holy God. He wants you to serve Him."

Moses entered the cloud. God called Moses to the mountain top. Moses stayed there for forty days while he talked to God. God explained to him all the laws of Israel. He told Moses all people need to obey these laws. God gave Moses two tablets made of stone to take back to the people. On these tablets God had written the Ten Commandments. Another word for commandment is covenant.

1. *Why were the people afraid?*
2. *What did God give Moses to take to the people?*

God Spoke These Words

Exodus 20:1-20

Moses listened to God for forty days. On the two tablets were the words God wanted the people to remember. God spoke these words:

Do not have any other Gods but me.
Do not worship false idols.
Do not take the name of the Lord in vain.
Always remember the Sabbath day to keep
    it holy.
Honor your father and mother.
Do not murder another.
Do not be with someone else's husband or
    wife.
Do not steal.
Do not bear false witness against your
    neighbor.
Do not desire your neighbor or anything
    the neighbor has.

When Moses returned from the mountain there was thunder and smoke. The people were afraid. Moses told the people not to be fearful, for God was testing them.

1. *What did Moses take with him from the mountain?*
2. *What did Moses tell the people God was doing?*

The Golden Calf

Exodus 32:1-8

Moses stayed on the mountain so long that the people thought something had happened to him. Was he alive? Did he run away?

Aaron, Moses brother, was a weak man. He encouraged the people to make a god of gold to worship. All of the people gave Aaron their gold. They gave him earrings and other gold items. He melted the gold and formed it into the shape of a calf. He announced, "Tomorrow there will be a festival." The next day the people sacrificed burnt offerings. They celebrated, danced and drank.

God knew what was happening. He told Moses to return to his people for they had become corrupt. "Remind them that I brought them out of Egypt, not false idols."

1. *What did Aaron encourage the Israelites to do?*
2. *Why was God mad at the people?*

Moses Destroys the Golden Calf

Exodus 32:9-34:4

Moses hurried down the mountain. He knew God was really mad. God threatened to destroy all of the people because they were worshipping false idols.

Moses begged God to change his mind. He asked God to remember Abraham, Isaac, and Jacob. Moses finally convinced God not to destroy the Israelites.

As Moses reached the bottom of the mountain he looked down and could see the party. He saw the gold calf and the dancers. He was mad and angry. He threw the stone tablets on the ground. They shattered into tiny pieces.

Moses went straight to the gold calf. First he smashed it. The he burned it and ground it into dust. Moses then told the people that the idol worshippers must be killed. Over 3,000 were killed that day. Moses went back to the Lord. "My people have sinned against you," he prayed, "but I asked that you forgive them."

"Lead the people to the place I have told you," God answered, "but there will come a time when the people will be punished." The Lord also told Moses to carve two new tablets just like the two that were broken. After carving the two stones, Moses went back up to the top of the mountain.

1. *Were the people faithful to God while Moses was gone?*
2. *What did Moses do to the golden calf?*

The Light on Moses' Face

Exodus 34:10-35:1

Once again Moses climbed to the top of the mountain. This time he took with him the two tablets as God had told him to do. Once again Moses spent forty days with God. God said to Moses, "I have made a covenant with you and with Israel." He told Moses about his laws. He wrote on the tablets the words of the covenant—the Ten Commandments.

When Moses came down from the mountain, he did not know that his face shone with God's light. The Israelites were frightened of Moses because his face was so full of God's radiance. They could not look at him. Moses called for them to come near. He spoke to the Israelites about God's law. Moses told the people, "These are the things God has commanded of you."

1. *Why did Moses face shine?*
2. *What were the words written on the tablets called?*

The Tabernacle I

Exodus 35-40

God was living among the people. He showed Moses how to build a special tent to be used for worship. It was called a tabernacle.

God told Moses to have everyone bring something for the tabernacle. The things that were needed were gold, silver, brass, animal skins, oil, bright-colored cloth, and precious stones.

The people were excited to have God with them. They willingly gave their precious items for the tabernacle. The women wove beautiful cloth. The men brought fine animal skins. They gave gold and silver jewelry. Those who could brought jewels, spices and oil.

Carpenters agreed to build. All who were able came to help build the tent for the meetings. God chose two wise men, Bezaleel and Aholiab, to teach the people to carve, engrave and weave. They all worked together to make everything for this place of worship.

In these days people lived in tents that could easily be moved from one camp to another. The tabernacle was to be built so that it could be moved as the people continued to journey toward Canaan.

The Israelites worked faithfully until the tabernacle was completed. God instructed Moses to set up the tabernacle in the middle of camp. The glory of the Lord filled the tabernacle.

1. *What were some of the things the people brought to build the tabernacle?*
2. *What was the tabernacle used for?*

The Tabernacle II

Exodus 35-40

Although the tabernacle was beautiful, it was not as ornate as the palaces of the kings of the time. God's home was simple but brilliant. Much of the beauty came because of the work the people put into it.

The tabernacle stood in the middle of the camp. Inside the tabernacle were two rooms. One was called the Holy Room. In the Holy Room were a gold table, a gold lampstand, and the Golden Altar of Incense.

The inner room was called the Holy of Holies. It was so sacred that no one but the high priest entered. It held the ark of the covenant, a gold box. Inside it were the two stone tablets where the words of God were written. It was in this room that God would dwell.

1. *How many rooms were in the tabernacle?*
2. *What was in the ark of the covenant?*

The Priests

Exodus 27:20-28:5

God chose Aaron and his sons to be priests of Israel. They would lead the worship and serve him. The high priest wore a robe and hat. There were stones on his robe. The priests did not wear shoes.

The priests regularly filled the lamps on the lampstand with oil. The lamps were never allowed to go out. The gold-covered table always held twelve fresh loaves of unleavened bread which represented an offering from each of the twelve tribes. The candlestick held seven burning lights. The small altar held incense. Everything in the room was made of gold or covered with gold.

Aaron and his sons were members of the tribe of Levi. The men from this tribe became the priest's helpers.

1. *What were some of the things in the tent?*
2. *Aaron and his sons were members of what tribe?*

The Scapegoat

Leviticus 16:7-10

One day a year was called the day of atonement. To take away the people's sins sacrifices were made of animals.

First the high priest sacrificed an ox. The priest must have his sins forgiven before asking for forgiveness for others.

Then the priest returned to the altar before the tabernacle. Two goats were brought to the entrance of the tent. One goat stood for the people of Israel and their sins. This goat was killed as a sacrifice to God for those sins. The second goat was a "scapegoat." A scapegoat is someone who takes the blame for something that someone else did. The goat was led so far into the wilderness that he could never find his way back to the camp. He was set free in the wilderness. This was to show how the sins of the people were taken away, never to come back again.

God wanted the people to know that sin was not good. But sins can be forgiven.

1. *Why were the animals sacrificed?*
2. *What was a scapegoat?*

The Twelve Spies

Numbers 13-14

Moses and his people had camped for almost a year near Mount Sinai. God's cloud had lifted from the tabernacle. It was time to continue the journey to Canaan.

They carefully packed the tent of meeting. Once again they followed the cloud left by God. At last they arrived outside of Canaan.

The Lord told Moses to pick one man from each tribe to spy in Canaan. Moses told the twelve to look over the land. Each was to bring back some fruit of the land.

For forty days the spies wandered through the Promised land. When they returned they brought back all kinds of beautiful food. There was fruit such as grapes. There were assorted vegetables. Never before had the people seen such food. The land was truly rich.

Caleb, one of the spies, wanted to go at once and take the land. But ten of the spies were fearful. One said, "The men of that land are so big they make us look like grasshoppers."

The people whined and worried. They forgot the promises God had made. The Israelites refused to go into the Promised Land.

1. *What did the spies bring back?*
2. *What did the spies tell the people that made them afraid?*

Back to the Desert

Numbers 14:1-45

Once again the people of Israel were complaining. "We should have stayed in Egypt." "We will die in the desert." "Why should we go to war with Canaan?"

Joshua and Caleb, the two spies who thought the people should go into Canaan, spoke to the people. They reminded the Israelites that if God was at their side they could do anything. "Do not be afraid if the Lord is with you."

Then God appeared to the Israelites, "How long will you disobey me? How long will you refuse to believe me? I have given you miracles, but still you do not believe. You will go back to the desert and wander for forty years."

The people said they would go to Canaan now. But Moses told the people, "You must not go, for God will not be with you." The people did not obey. They went to Canaan and many Israelites were killed.

As God had spoken, they traveled the desert for forty years. God had promised no one could go into Canaan until the older generation who did not have faith in him died. Only the younger generation and Caleb and Joshua would be allowed to enter.

1. *Why was God mad at the people?*
2. *How long did they travel through the desert?*

The Brass Snake

Numbers 21:4-9

The people traveled along the Red Sea. They spoke against God. They spoke against Moses. "We have no bread!" "The water is not good." "We dislike the food."

God was very angry. He sent poisonous snakes to bite many of the people who complained. Some of the people died.

The people knew they had sinned. They went to Moses for help. Moses prayed for his people. God told Moses to make a snake out of brass. Moses was to place the snake on a pole. Anyone who was bitten by a snake could look at the pole. That person would not die.

Moses did as he was told. From then on anyone bitten by a snake would look at the brass snake on the pole and the snake bite would heal.

1. *Do you think God and Moses got tired of hearing the people complain?*
2. *What did God do because the people complained?*

Moses' Death

Deuteronomy 31:1-34

Already God had told Moses that he would not lead the Israelites into the Promised Land. It was time for the people to cross the Jordan. It was near time for Moses to die. He was 120 years old.

Moses called the leaders of the twelve tribes to his tent. He told them all of the things God had done for their fathers. He gave them the words of God's law. He told them it was important for all of the people to keep God's laws as well as teach the laws to their children.

The Word was never to be forgotten.

God had chosen Joshua to take Moses place as leader of the people. He laid his hands on Joshua's head. Both men felt God's presence.

While the people wept, Moses left the camp alone. He walked up the mountainside. He look out over the Promised Land which would soon belong to his people. There was the Jordan River. He saw the Dead Sea. Jericho was surrounded by a high wall. He could see where Abraham, Isaac, and Jacob were buried.

Moses died on the mountaintop. No man ever lived as close to God as Moses until God's son, Jesus, lived among men.

1. *Do you think Moses was sad about not leading the people into the Promised Land?*
2. *Who did God tell to lead the Israelites into the Promised Land?*

Crossing the Jordan

Joshua 3:1-5:12

Joshua led the Israelites to the edge of the Jordan River. Once they crossed the river they would be in the Promised Land. At the front of the people were the priests with the ark. The could see the beautiful pastures, the green hills, and the golden grain on the other side.

There was often deep waters this time of the year. The people camped on the edge of the river and waited for the water to go down.

After waiting three days, the officers went through the camp to tell all of the people to watch for the priests. When the time was right the priests, carrying the ark of the Lord, would lead the Israelites across the river. The people were warned to be ready.

The next day God told Joshua, "As I was with Moses, I will be with you. The people shall see it. Tell the priests to go with the ark to the edge of the river and wait." They did as the Lord had said.

When the priests touched the edge of the water, the water stopped flowing. The priests and the people crossed the Jordan on dry land. The Israelites made camp near Jericho. None of this generation of people had eaten anything but manna. The found fruits and vegetables and enjoyed the good food of Canaan. Manna never fell again.

1. *What did God do to help the people cross the swollen river?*
2. *What did the people eat for the first time?*

Rahab Helps the Israelites

Joshua 2:1-24

Across the Jordan River, several miles from the camp of the Israelites, was the city of Jericho. There was a high wall around Jericho. Everyone came and went through a gate.

The people in Jericho had been hearing about what God was doing for the Israelites.

They knew God helped the Israelites fight their enemies.

Two of the Israelites spent the night with a woman from Jericho named Rahab. When the king of Jericho heard this he sent soldiers to capture them. Rahab hid the Israelites. She sent the soldiers away to look for them elsewhere.

Rahab was concerned about her family. She knew God was protecting the Israelites. "Please promise you will not hurt my family," she pleaded. "Since you saved our life, we will protect you," stated the Israelites. "Leave a red cord in the window. All will know to pass the house with this sign."

1. *What did Rahab do for the spies?*
2. *What did the spies promise Rahab?*

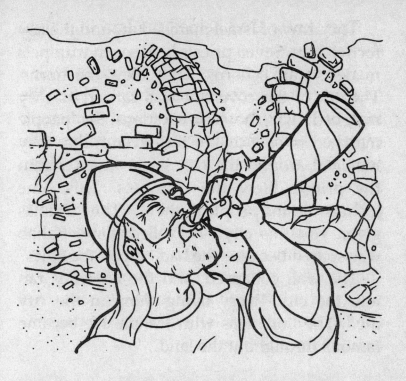

The Fall of the Wall at Jericho

Joshua 6:27

No one could enter or leave Jericho because of the Israelites. God told Joshua the city of Jericho would belong to the Israelites. He told Joshua how to defeat the city.

The army of Israel marched around the city for six days. Seven priests held seven trumpets made of ram's horns. They blew the horns. The ark of the covenant was carried as they marched. For the first six days the people marched in silence. On the seventh day they marched around the city seven times. Again the priests blew the trumpets. This time Joshua told the people to shout. "The Lord has given you this city," he yelled. Only Rahab was spared because she had helped the spies.

The wall collapsed, and the Israelites ran into the city. Every living thing in the city died. The Lord was with Joshua. He became famous throughout the land.

1. *Who made the plan of defeat toward Jericho?*
2. *Who blew the trumpets?*

Joshua Is Tricked

Joshua 9:1-27

Many of the people in the area came together to make war against Israel. The people of Gibeon decided to try a different approach.

Strange men in old ragged clothes came to see Joshua. "We have come from a far country. We know you have been taking over towns as you did Jericho. We know about your great God. We want to be your friends and live with you in peace."

Joshua and his officers felt sorry for the men. They must have come a long way. They saw no reason to speak with God about these men. They promised peace to the Gibeonites.

Three days later the Israelites came to Gibeon. They learned the strangers were from this land so close to them. They had promised to let these people live. They felt very foolish. They had been tricked.

When Joshua asked the people of Gibeon why they had lied, they replied they were afraid after they heard what had happened at Jericho.

Joshua told the people they had to be punished because they had lied. They were to serve Israel from that day forward. They would not own land or houses. They would cut the wood and carry water for Israel.

1. *What mistake did Joshua make when the Gibeonites came to him?*
2. *How did Joshua solve the problem of the Gibeonites?*

The Israelites Have More Battles

Joshua 10:1-11:23

The largest city in the area was Jerusalem. The people in Jerusalem worshiped idols. Four other cities joined with the king of Jerusalem to destroy Gibeon. This meant that five kings were working together to ruin Gibeon, and the Israelites along with it. All from the other cities were upset that Gibeon had made peace with Israel.

The people of Gibeon went to Joshua for help. They knew they could not fight the five kings alone.

Joshua called together his army. They marched all night. When they came upon the five kings there was a great battle. The Lord said to Joshua, "Do not be afraid. Be brave and lead your people." The Lord brought hailstones on the enemy which killed more people than swords.

The five kings and their armies were destroyed by the Israelites. With this victory the south of Canaan was won. Joshua then turned his army. He led his army against more kings from the north.

Even after all of these victories, it would still be a long time before all of the land was taken by the Israelites.

1. What did the people of Jerusalem worship?
2. Why did the king of Jerusalem want to attack the Gibeonites?

Dividing the Land

Joshua 15:1-19:51

God told Joshua to divide the land tribe by tribe. There were twelve tribes of Israel, one for each of the sons of Jacob. Two tribes and half of another already had their land. Their land was on the east of the Jordan. This left nine and one-half tribes to receive their share of land.

The land was divided. The tribe of Ephraim was in the middle country. This was an area with rich soil and many springs and streams of water. It was on this land near Mount Ebal that Joseph was finally buried. His coffin of stone had been held since they left Egypt forty years before. Ephraim was a son of Joseph. Joshua lived in Ephraim because he also belonged to that tribe.

The land had always been called Canaan. Now it was to be called the Land of Israel.

1. Why was the land divided into twelve parts?
2. What was the new name of the land?

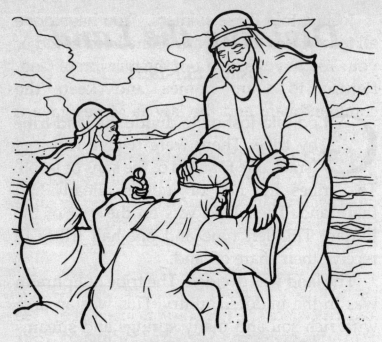

The Altar by the Jordan

Joshua 22:1-34

The tribes broke camp at Gilgal where they had met during the conquest of Canaan. They departed to go to their new land. Joshua called a meeting of the soldiers of the two and one-half tribes who had received their land on the east of the Jordan.

Joshua told these soldiers, "You have done all that Moses the servant of the Lord asked of you. You have carried out the mission of God. Return to your homes and keep the commandment and the law as Moses gave it to you."

Joshua blessed them and sent them across the river to their families. Joshua had set the tabernacle up in Shiloh. All of the people came there to worship. The tribes on the east of the Jordan decided to set up another altar.

The other tribes were upset. "Why do you set up another altar? Do you rebel against God and His wishes?" The soldiers answered, "We want our children to see it standing on your side of the river. It is a reminder that we are all one people divided by the river Jordan. We all worship the one God of Israel."

1. Why were the tribes upset about the new altar?
2. What was the reason the new altar was built by the river?

Joshua's Farewell

Joshua 23-24

For many years the Israelites built homes and cities. They enjoyed the land God had given them.

Joshua was now more than 100 years old. He wanted to talk to the people one more time, so he called the leaders of the twelve tribes together. Joshua reminded them what God had done for them and for their fathers. He told them the stories of their ancestors from Abraham forward. He said, "Keep all of God's laws that Moses gave you. Serve the Lord with your heart."

The people understood. Joshua wanted the people to be reminded of their promise when he was gone. He set up a huge stone under an oak tree at Shechem. He told the people the stone represented the fact that God heard their promise. From that day forward whenever the people saw that stone, they remembered their promise to God and Joshua.

1. *Why did Joshua want to talk to the people before he died?*
2. *What did Joshua build to remind the people of their promise?*

Israel Forgets the Lord

Judges 1:1-3:7

Years later the older people worshiped God, but the younger ones had forgotten Him. God told Israel to make the people living in Canaan leave. No one did this.

The Canaanites worshiped idols and false gods. Many of the younger Israelites began to worship the gods of the Canaanites. They quit going to the tabernacle.

This made God very angry. He decided to let Israel suffer. Sometimes their enemies attacked them. They were poor because their enemies robbed them of their grain, olive oil, grapes, and even their animals.

The Israelites would suffer and then they would remember God. He would send a wise person called a judge who would save them. But then they would again worship idols. God would again send a judge who would help, but again they would forget God when the judge died. For 300 years after Joshua died, this happened many times.

1. *Why did the people worship false gods?*
2. *Who were the judges?*

Deborah, The Judge

Judges 4:1-7

There was one judge who was a woman. Her name was Deborah. She was the only woman to ever rule the Israelites. She sat under a palm tree near Jerusalem and gave advice to the people who came to her. She was very wise. Everyone came to her to solve their problems. Deborah had God's Spirit with her. This is why people listened to her and took her advice.

There was a Canaanite king named Jabin who attacked Israel. Deborah sent for a brave man living in the land of Naphtali named Barak. She sent for him to lead the army of Israel. She told him God would help him defeat Jabin's army.

1. Why was Deborah chosen to be a judge?
2. Why did she send for Barak?

Deborah and Jael

Judges 4:8-24

Barak went to Deborah. She was speaking for the Lord. Barak was afraid. He told Deborah he would not go into battle unless she went with him. She agreed to go with him, but she said since he did not trust God, the victory of the war would belong to a woman.

They put out a call for men to help with the battle. Ten thousand men came. This was still a small army compared to the Canaanite army.

Deborah sent Barak to attack. The Canaanites were not prepared. They were frightened. The Canaanites were not organized. They started running. Chariots and horses went in many directions. The Lord made the river flood. Many of the enemies died in the flood. The Canaanite general, Sisera, ran away on his chariot. He stopped at a tent which belonged to a woman named Jael. She let him hide under a rug. He fell asleep. Jael knew he was the enemy. She crept in to the tent while Sisera was asleep. She took a tent peg and hammered it into the side of his head. Sisera died.

Jael and Deborah set the people of Israel free by showing their bravery.

1. *Who was Barak?*
2. *Who killed Sisera?*

Gideon and God

Judges 6:1-32

Again the people of Israel turned to evil ways. So the Lord again made them suffer. For seven years the Midianites pushed their way across the land occupied by Israel. They took pastures and water for their cattle. They stole food from the fields. The valleys were full of Midianite tents.

The Israelites were hungry and unhappy. They had been pushed from their land. Yet again they cried to God for help.

One day a man named Gideon was threshing wheat. He saw a man sitting under a tree. The man said to him, "Gideon, the Lord is with you. You are a brave man. Go forth and save your people from the Midianites." Gideon answered, "Sir, I am from a poor family and I am the youngest. How could I save Israel?"

"I will be with you and I will help you," the man answered. Gideon then realized he was talking to God.

He gathered ten men and that night they destroyed the altar which held the idols. He built an altar and prepared a burnt offering to God. The next day the people saw the new altar. At first they were mad, but then they felt foolish for worshipping such a god.

1. *Who did Gideon see sitting under a tree?*
2. *Why did Gideon think he could not help his people?*

Gideon's Small Army

Judges 7:1-15

Thirty-two thousand soldiers gathered to help Gideon defeat the Midianites. God told Gideon his army was too big. "When the Midianites are defeated, the Israelites will think it was won because of their own power. I want them to know my power. Tell all of the men who are afraid to go home." Over 22,000 men went away.

With 10,000 soldiers left God told Gideon the army was still too big. God told Gideon to call the men together. He told Gideon how to divide the army until only the best and bravest soldiers were left.

Gideon told the soldiers to march down the hill as if they were going to be attacked. He marched them by the water. When they stopped to drink, some put down the spears and shields and drank with both hands. Some kept spear and shield in one hand and scooped water with the other hand. They were ready for the enemy even while drinking water.

God told Gideon to take only those men who had stayed prepared. Those soldiers who kept spears and shields in one hand and drank with the other were chosen to set Israel free. There were only 300 of them, but all were brave, sincere men who were always prepared.

That night God told Gideon to go to the enemy camp and listen. At the camp of the Midianites Gideon heard one soldier tell another of a dream. "I dreamed a loaf of bread hit my tent and knocked it down. What does that mean?" The other soldier said, "It is the sword of the mighty Gideon. God has given us to him."

Gideon was pleased at what he heard. He knew the Midianites feared him. He gave thanks to God. He then returned to camp to prepare for the battle.

1. *Why did God send away part of Gideon's army?*
2. *What was the meaning of the dream of the Midianite?*

Gideon's Dream

Judges 7:16-8:28

Gideon divided his army into three companies. Each soldier was given a pitcher with a lamp burning inside and a trumpet. After dark the soldiers quietly walked down the mountain. Gideon arranged them all around the Midianite camp.

When all were in place, the pitchers were broken and there was a flash of light. There was light all around the camp. The soldiers blew the trumpets all at once. Then the soldiers shouted, "The sword of the Lord and of Gideon!"

The Midianites were very frightened at the light and the sound of the trumpets. Instead of fighting they ran away. They trampled each other. They fought among themselves. They were even killing each other.

Gideon sent men to the nearby tribes to warn them of the fleeing Midianites. The tribe of Ephraim stopped the Midianites at the Jordan River. They never fought with Israel again.

Gideon was a judge for forty years. For all of this time there was peace in Israel. The people asked him to be their king, but Gideon told the people that only the Lord God was king. During these years there were fifteen judges over Israel. Gideon, the fifth judge, had the most courage, wisdom, and faith

1. *What did Gideon's army take with them into battle?*
2. *Why did Gideon refuse to be king?*

Jephthah Leads Israel to Victory

Judges 10:6-11:40

Jephthah lived in the land of Tob. He was a strong man. He was known for his good deeds. The Israelites were in trouble again. After Gideon died they quit worshipping God.

This time from the east came the Ammonites to rule over the Israelites. God decided to let the Israelites fight their own battle. He was weary of their serving other gods. The people prayed to God. They destroyed the idols. They knew only God could save them.

Jephthah was called to lead the Israelites to freedom. Jephthah made a very foolish promise before he went into battle. "God please give me victory in this battle. If you do, I will sacrifice the first who greets me when I return home."

Jephthah had a great victory over the Ammonites. He drove them out of the land. When he returned home it was his only child, a daughter, who came out to meet him. Jephthah was upset. He knew his promise was a bad one. His daughter lived for two months before she told her dad it was time to fulfill his promise to God. This was the only time during the history of the Israelites that a living person was offered in sacrifice to God.

1. *What did Jephthah promise God?*
2. *Who greeted Jephthah when he returned home?*

Samson

Judges 13:1-14:4

Over and over the Israelites worshiped idols. So God gave them to their enemies. This was by far the hardest and longest oppression. The enemy was the Philistines. They worshiped an idol called Dagon. This god had a man's body with a head of a fish.

The Philistines took the Israelites' swords and spears. Now they couldn't fight. They robbed Israel of their crops. The people cried to God. God listened.

An angel came to a woman and said, "You will have a son who will save Israel. Make sure your son never drinks wine. His hair must grow long."

The child soon came. He was named Samson. Samson grew up to become the strongest of men. He never had an army. He helped his people alone. Samson met a Philistine woman. He told his father he wanted to marry her. His parents were not happy that he would want to marry a Philistine. They did not know that this marriage would help free Israel from the Philistines.

1. *How was Samson different from other leaders?*
2. *Why were his parents upset about his choice for a wife?*

Samson and the Lion

Judges 14:5-9

Samson went to Timnah with his mother and father. As they reached the vineyards, a young lion came roaring toward Samson. The spirit of the Lord was with Samson. It gave him the strength to tear the lion apart with his hands. He did not tell his mother or father what he had done.

Later he returned to Timnah for his wedding. He passed the dead lion. He saw that bees had made a nest in the lion. There was honey in the hive. He scooped the honey with his hands and ate it as he walked along. He gave honey to his mother and father, but he did not tell them it came from the dead lion.

1. *Where did Samson get the strength to kill the lion?*
2. *What did he find in the lion?*

Samson at the Wedding

Judges 14:10-20

Samson continued to his wedding. As was the tradition there would be a wedding feast which would last a week.

After the wedding Samson told thirty young men, "I have a riddle for you. If you can give me the answer before the wedding feast is over, I will give you a shirt and cloak. If you do not know the answer, you must give me a shirt and cloak." The young men were sure that in seven days they could guess the answer to the riddle.

Out of the eater, something to eat.
Out of the strong, something sweet.

The young Philistines could not guess the answer to the riddle. They threatened Samson's wife. They told her they would burn the home of her family if she did not learn the answer to the riddle.

She cried and pleaded with Samson until he told her the story of the lion and the honey. Samson's wife immediately told the Philistines. The Philistines came to Samson with the answer to the riddle. Samson had to pay them the clothes.

With the Lord's spirit Samson killed thirty Philistines for their clothes. Filled with anger, Samson returned to his father's home without his wife. Samson's wife was given to a friend who was at the wedding.

1. *How did the young Philistines learn the answer to the riddle?*
2. *Where did Samson get the clothes to give the Philistines?*

Samson and the Philistines

Judges 15:1-20

It was now time to harvest the wheat. Samson was sorry his anger had overcome him during the wedding feast. He decided to visit his wife. But her father had already given her in marriage to someone else.

Again Samson was angry. On the way home he caught three hundred foxes, tied their tails together two by two, and attached a lit torch to the tails. The foxes ran through the fields and destroyed the crops.

The Philistines took an army to capture Samson. The camped in Judah. They convinced the men of Judah to catch Samson and tie him up. They turned Samson over to the Philistines. But the spirit of the Lord was with Samson. With the strength he received from the Lord, he broke the ropes.

Samson grabbed the jawbone of a donkey which was on the ground. He started swinging. That day Samson killed 1,000 Philistines.

He was very thirsty. He cried out to the Lord for water. The Lord brought water up from the ground. Samson led Israel for twenty years.

1. *Why were the Philistines trying to capture Samson?*
2. *How did Samson defeat the Philistines?*

Samson and Delilah

Judges 16:4-30

Samson knew the Philistines hated him. But he also knew they were afraid to hurt him. Samson was now in love with a Philistine woman named Delilah. He visited her often.

When the Philistine rulers realized he was seeing Delilah, they went to see her. They promised her many pieces of silver if she could learn the secret to his strength.

Delilah tried several times to trick Samson into telling her the secret to his strength. He always teased her. He would tell her things which were not true. Delilah became mad. She told Samson he was making a fool of her. She nagged him day after day.

He finally told her everything. "God set me apart at birth. I am a Nazirite. I have never had my hair cut. If my head were shaved, I would have no strength." That night Delilah held Samson's head while he went to sleep. While he was asleep she had a man cut off his hair. When he awoke he had no strength.

The Philistines grabbed him, gouged out his eyes and put him in prison. Samson's hair grew back while he was in prison.

One night while the Philistines were having a feast they brought Samson in to perform for them. Samson asked to be placed where he could feel the pillars that supported the temple. He quietly prayed to God to give him strength one more time. He wanted revenge on the Philistines. He pushed with all of his might. He knocked over the pillars which supported the temple. Samson died with the Philistines, but that day he killed more Philistines than he had while he lived.

1. *Why did Delilah want to know the secret of Samson's strength?*
2. *What did Samson do to the Philistines?*

Naomi and Ruth

Ruth 1:1-19

There was a famine in the land during the time that the judges ruled. A man named Elimelech took his wife and two sons from Bethlehem near Judah to Moab. They were trying to find a better life. While in Moab, Elimelech died. The two sons had married Moab women named Orpah and Ruth. After they had lived there about ten years, both of the sons died.

Naomi decided to return to her people. She told her daughters-in-law to return to their people. She kissed them and wished them well. Orpah bid her mother-in-law good-bye. Ruth turned to Naomi to hug her.

"Where you go I will go, and where you stay I will stay. Your people will be my people and your God my God. Where you die I will die. May the Lord deal with me."

The two returned to Bethlehem together.

1. *Why did Elimelech and his family move to Moab?*
2. *Who stayed with Naomi and what was her famous promise?*

Ruth's Story

Ruth 2:1-4:22

Naomi had a relative on her husband's side name Boaz who owned fields of grain. The Israelites always left some grain standing. This was called gleanings and was left for the poor.

Ruth went to glean the fields of Boaz. Boaz gave Ruth water and told her to continue in his fields. He also gave her food for lunch.

Ruth worked hard that day. She returned to Naomi with her riches from the fields. She told Naomi of the rich man. Naomi told Ruth that he was part of her family.

There was a feast at the end of the harvest. Ruth went to Boaz as Ruth had suggested.

She asked him to be kind to her and Naomi.

Boaz soon fell in love with Ruth. They were married. Naomi went to live with Ruth and her family. Boaz and Ruth had a son named Obed. Obed had a son named Jesse. Jesse was the father of David, a king of Israel. Ruth, the young woman of Moab, became the mother of a king of Israel.

1. *Why was Ruth gleaning the fields?*
2. *Who was related to Ruth and Boaz?*

Hannah Shares Samuel

1 Samuel 1:1-2:26

While Eli was a judge in Israel, there was a man who lived there named Elkanah who had two wives. One wife had children. The other wife, named Hannah, had no children.

Hannah cried and prayed to the Lord. She told the Lord that if she could have a son she would give him back to be raised as a Nazirite priest.

The Lord heard Hannah's prayer. She had a baby boy that she named Samuel, which means "asked of God." While Samuel was still very young Hannah took him to Eli who was also a priest. "God gave me this special child. I promised I would teach him to serve the Lord. Let him grow up in God's house here with you."

Samuel helped the old priest. Eli's own sons were rascals who fell out of favor with their father. But Samuel continued to grow in stature with the Lord and with all men.

1. *What was Hannah's prayer to God?*
2. *What did she name her child Samuel?*

Samuel Hears God Speak

1 Samuel 3:1-21

One night Samuel was lying down in the temple when he heard a voice. He thought it was Eli. Eli told him he had not called out. A second and third time the boy heard a voice. Eli finally realized it was God calling to Samuel. Eli told the boy that when the voice called again he was to answer, "Speak, Lord, for your servant is listening."

That night God told Samuel that he was going to punish Eli's family. Eli's sons had been very wicked. Eli did not punish them even though he knew they were doing evil. The Lord said, "I will do something in Israel that will make the ears of everyone tingle."

Samuel was sad. He was afraid to tell Eli what God had said. He stayed in his room to avoid Eli. Eli finally called to him. "Samuel, my son, what was it the Lord said to you last night?" Samuel told Eli all that the Lord said. Eli replied, "He is the Lord, let him do what he should."

The Lord was with Samuel as he grew up. He revealed himself to Samuel through his word.

1. *Who called out to Samuel in the night?*
2. *Why did God curse Eli's family?*

God's Ark Is Captured

1 Samuel 4:1-22

The Israelites went to fight the Philistines. Over 4,000 Israelites were killed on the battlefield. They were defeated. The Israel chiefs were confused that the Lord let the Philistines win.

The Israelites decided to bring the ark of the covenant from Shiloh. They felt if they brought it God would be with them.

Eli's two sons were priests in Shiloh. They cared for the ark of the covenant. They allowed the warriors to take it into battle.

The Philistines and Israelites fought again. This time Israel lost 30,000 soldiers. The ark of God was captured, and Eli's two sons died.

Eli was an old man. He stayed in Shiloh sitting by the gate during the battle. He was worried about the ark. A man came running in from the battle with news for all. He saw Eli and went to him to tell him the news. Upon hearing that his sons were dead and the ark had been captured, Eli fell over in his chair. He died from a broken neck. The glory had departed from Israel.

1. *Why was the ark removed from Shiloh?*
2. *What happened to Eli when he heard the news from the battle?*

A King for the Israelites

1 Samuel 8:1-9:25

The Philistines returned the ark of the covenant after seven months. Samuel was judge and Israel was at peace. The people were serving the Lord. But the twelve tribes wanted a king.

Samuel was afraid a king would turn Israel from God. But God spoke to him. "Listen to all that the people are saying to you. They do not reject you but me as their king. They have rejected me since I brought them out of Egypt. Warn them how a king will rule over them."

Saul, a wealthy Benjaminite, was a young man. God had told Samuel to make a man from Benjamin the king of Israel. God knew Saul could save his people from the Philistines. Samuel took Saul to a feast. He told Saul he would serve God in a special way.

The next day Samuel told Saul that God had chosen him to rule as king over Israel. Samuel then anointed Saul by pouring a flask of oil over his head. Samuel wrote rules for the kingship on a scroll and left it in the tabernacle. Judges had ruled Israel for 300 years. Now there would be a king.

1. *Why didn't Samuel want Israel to have a king?*
2. *Who was the first king of Israel?*

Saul Takes Control

1 Samuel 11:1-12:25

Saul continued to work in his fields even after Samuel anointed him as king. Saul was working one day when a man came running by with news. The Ammonites had attacked Jabesh in Giliad.

The man told Saul that there had not been enough Israelites in the city to fight. They had told the Ammonites that if they could live the Ammonites could rule them. The Ammonite king had threatened to put out the right eye of each person in the town. Israel wept.

Saul burned with anger. The Spirit of the Lord came to him. He cut an oxen into pieces and sent them through the land. With the pieces Saul sent the message, "Follow Saul and Samuel to fight against the Ammonites or this is what will be done to your oxen." Saul had over 300,000 soldiers that fought with him in his victory.

Samuel called all of the people to Gilgal. Gilgal was where Joshua had first camped in Canaan. Samuel reminded all what God had done for them. They offered sacrifices to God, and Samuel turned over the kingdom. Samuel said, "I will always pray for you. You now have a king, but you must continue to obey and serve the Lord. If you do evil, you and your king will be swept away."

1. *Why was Saul upset when he heard the Ammonites had taken over Jabesh?*
2. *What did Samuel tell the people to remember?*

Saul Disobeys God

1 Samuel 15:1-35

Samuel told Saul that it was God's will for him to go and totally destroy the Amalekites. Saul was to destroy everything that belonged to them.

Saul took his army and demolished the city but they saved all that was good such as animals. They would use the animals for sacrifices. Word of Saul's actions came to Samuel. He was worried and prayed to God.

Samuel joined Saul. He asked why Saul disobeyed God's command. Saul thought he did what God had asked. Samuel told Saul, "Obedience to God is far more important than sacrifices. God told you to destroy everything. He will reject you as king." As Samuel turned to leave Saul grabbed Samuel's coat and ripped it. "Just as you have torn my coat, God will rip his kingdom from you to give it to a better man," sighed Samuel. Samuel continued to mourn for Saul, but the two never saw each other again.

1. *What did God tell Saul to do about the Amalekites?*
2. *Why did God take his kingdom from Saul?*

David—The Chosen One

1 Samuel 16:1-13

God told Samuel to fill his flask with oil and go to Jesse of Bethlehem. "I have chosen one of his sons to be king."

At Bethlehem Samuel offered God a sacrifice. Jesse was there with his seven sons. Samuel told Jesse that one would be anointed. "The Lord does not look at what man looks at. Man looks at the outward appearance, but God looks at the heart." Samuel looked at the sons and then asked Jesse, "Do you have another son?" "Yes," Jesse answered, "My youngest son, David, is with the sheep."

Jesse sent for David. When he arrived Samuel told all that the Lord had chosen David. In the presence of his brothers Samuel anointed him. From that day forward David was filled with the Spirit of the Lord.

1. What does God look for in his chosen people?
2. Who was present when David was anointed?

David Plays for Saul

1 Samuel 16:14-23

While David was growing and praying to God, Saul lost the spirit and no longer obeyed God's word. Saul became unhappy and no longer was at peace with God. The people around Saul thought that he was cheered when he heard someone playing a harp.

One young man knew that Jesse of Bethlehem had a son who played a harp. Saul sent a message to Jesse to send his son to play.

David came and played his harp for Saul. It cheered him up and made him feel better. Saul was not aware that Samuel had anointed David. He would have been jealous if he had known.

After a time Saul seemed better, so David left him to return to being a shepherd.

1. Why was Saul full of sad feelings?
2. Why did Saul call for David to play for him?

David and Goliath

1 Samuel 17:1-51

Saul remained king for a while after David was anointed. While he was still king, the Philistines were still doing battle with the Israelites.

There was a Philistine named Goliath who was nine feet tall. He was very strong. Goliath sent the Israelites a challenge. He said he would fight any Israelite they chose. If he won the fight, Israel would be the servants of the Philistines. If the Israelite won, the Philistines would be servants.

David went to the camp to take food to three of his brothers who were in the army. Every day Goliath yelled the challenge to the Israelites. David took the challenge. He told his people, "Don't let him defy God's army!"

He went to the river and chose five smooth stones for his slingshot. With his shepherd's staff, slingshot and pouch of stones, he approached Goliath. He told Goliath, "You come with a sword and spears. I come in the name of the Lord."

Goliath bellowed, "You come to fight me with a stick! Do you think I am a dog?" David ran toward Goliath. He hurled a stone deep into the forehead of the giant. Goliath fell face down on the ground. David ran and stood over him. He knew he won a victory for Israel that day.

1. *Why were the Israelites afraid of Goliath?*
2. *What did David use to kill Goliath?*

King David

2 Samuel 6:1-7:16

David was thirty years old when Israel made him king. David decided to move the ark of the covenant to Jerusalem. He prepared a new tabernacle on Mount Zion. As the ark was moved on a cart drawn by oxen in route to Mount Zion, the people cheered and danced and sang.

Jerusalem became known as the City of David. For the first time in many years the priests offered sacrifices at the tabernacle each day.

David said to Nathan, who was a prophet, "I live in a cedar house, but the ark of God is still in a tent. It is time we built a home for the ark."

That night God spoke to Nathan. He told Nathan to tell David, "I have never asked my people to build me a house. I am glad you, the shepherd, thought to build a house for the ark. You are a good leader with great power. Because you have done my will, I will see that your son sits on the throne. He shall build me a house and a temple. I will give your descendants a kingdom which will last forever."

This promise from God was fulfilled with the birth of Jesus who was from the house of David.

1. *What did David decide must be done with the ark of the covenant?*
2. *How did God reward David for doing his will?*

Wise Solomon Is King

1 Kings 3:1-28

Solomon, David's son, became king at a very young age. He was not much more than twenty. Solomon prayed to God for wisdom and knowledge. God told him he would make him wiser than any king before or after him. God also told Solomon if he obeyed him, he would have a long life and rule for many years.

Soon after this Solomon had a chance to show his wisdom. Two women came to him with two babies. One was dead and the other alive. Both women claimed the living child as their own. Both argued in front of the king about the baby. Solomon listened for a while then asked for a sword. He held the baby up and said, "I will cut the child in two. Each of you may have half." One of the women screamed. "Please don't! Let the other woman have my child, but please, let my child live!" Solomon gave the child to the woman who would not let the child be killed. "She is truly its mother," he said.

People were amazed at his wisdom.

1. *What promise did God make Solomon?*
2. *How did Solomon show his wisdom with the two women?*

Solomon's Temple

1 Kings 5:1-9:9

The most important thing Solomon did while he was king was build the temple for God. It was built on Mount Moriah and covered the whole mountain.

The temple was made of stone and wood. All of the stones were cut before they were brought to Mount Moriah. They were cut to fit perfectly.

All of the beams for the roof and the pillars of cedar were carved and made to join each other. The cedar was cut from trees on Mount Lebanon. King Hiram, a friend of Solomon, ordered his men to cut the cedar trees, make them into rafts, then float them to Joppa. There they were carried to Jerusalem. There were no hammers used to build the temple. As the walls were built, there was no noise.

The temple was similar to the tabernacle, except it was much larger. It took seven years to build the temple. Once it was finished a service was held to dedicate it to the Lord. The ark was brought from Mount Zion and placed in the Holy of Holies. King Solomon offered a prayer to the Lord. All of the people filled the temple while he knelt in front of the altar.

Later the Lord appeared to Solomon and said, "I have heard your prayer. The temple shall be holy. My eyes and heart will always be there. If you do as your father, David, before you, you shall keep your throne. But if you turn away from the Lord, I will let the enemies of Israel destroy the temple."

1. *Tell how the temple was built.*
2. *What did God say about the temple?*

Elijah the Prophet

1 Kings 17:1-24

It was during the reign of King Ahab that the prophet Elijah from Gilead appeared. He went to King Ahab and told him that the Lord had told him that no dew or rain would fall until Elijah asked for it. He then hid himself as God had instructed.

No rain fell. The brook where Elijah was getting water for himself went dry. The Lord spoke to Elijah again. He told him to go to Zarephath where a widow would care for him.

When he arrived in Zarephath there was a woman by the gate picking up sticks. Elijah asked her for water and bread. She brought him water, but told him that she had only enough flour and oil for one loaf of bread. She must save it for her son and herself. Elijah told her that if she would make bread for him that the Lord would give her flour and oil until the rain came.

The widow believed Elijah. She shared with him. From that day on the woman had oil and flour in her jars every day.

One day her son became very sick. Before the day was over he died. The woman was upset and cried to Elijah, "Oh man of God, did you come here and cause my son to die?" Elijah told her to bring her son to him.

Elijah took the boy to his room and placed him on the bed. Elijah spoke to the Lord. "Oh Lord, why have you brought tragedy to this woman by taking her son?" He stretched his body across the boy three times, then cried to the Lord, "Please let this child live." The Lord heard Elijah's prayer. Life came into the body of the child. Elijah carried the boy downstairs to his mother. The woman said to Elijah, "Now I know you are a man of God. You speak the Lord's words."

1. *What did the woman do for Elijah?*
2. *What did Elijah do to bring the boy back to life?*

Nehemiah Builds the City

Nehemiah 1:1-3:32

Nehemiah was a cup bearer for the Persian King Artaxerxes. It was his job to choose the wine for the king's table, as well as serve it.

Nehemiah loved Jerusalem more than anything. When he heard that the walls of Jerusalem were down and that her gates had been burned, he was very unhappy. He prayed to God to help him find a way to rebuild Jerusalem. He promised God he would talk to the king.

When next he served the king some wine, the king noticed his sadness. He asked, "Are you sick? Why are you so sad?"

Nehemiah told the king about Jerusalem. He asked the king to let him go to Judea to rebuild the city. The king gave him permission to go.

Nehemiah rode a thousand miles to Jerusalem. He told the men with him. "Come, let us rebuild Jerusalem. Then we will have respect. We have the good will of the king." All of the families in Jerusalem agreed to build a part of the wall. Priests, rich and poor helped build the wall. Those living near by such as Ammonites and Ashdodites were angry. They did not want the city to be strong.

It took fifty-two days to finish. The gates were closed. Guards stood by. They all knew that God helped build the wall.

1. *What favor did Nehemiah ask of the king?*
2. *Who helped the Jews build the wall?*

Reading the Law

Nehemiah 8:1-12

The Israelites settled into their towns. They decided to assemble in the square before the Water Gate. They asked Ezra the scribe to bring out the Book of the Law of Moses.

Ezra brought out the Law. All of the men and women listened from daybreak until noon. He stood on a wooden platform. Ezra praised the Lord. All of the people lifted their hands and said, "Amen, amen." He read the Law clearly so the people could understand the words.

They bowed down and worshipped the Lord. They started to weep. Nehemiah said, "Do not mourn or weep. Go eat and drink. Send some to those who have nothing. The joy of the Lord is your strength." This was a sacred day.

So the people went away to eat and drink and celebrate. They now understood the words of the Lord.

1. *What was Ezra asked to do?*
2. *What did the people do when the Law was read?*

Beautiful Queen Esther

Esther 1:1-2

When King Darius died, his son Ahasuerus claimed the throne. He was not wise like his father. For 180 days after he became king he celebrated with all of the nobles and priests. For the last seven days a banquet was held, and Ahasuerus drank too much wine. He wanted to show off his beautiful queen, Vashti. She was shy. She did not think it wise to walk in front of the men.

The king was angry that Vashti disobeyed him. An adviser told him that when the women in the land heard that his wife had been disrespectful, that all women would behave the same. The king was advised to find another queen to take her place.

The king put out a decree that the most beautiful young women in the kingdom should be brought to the palace.

There was a young, Jewish girl named Esther whose parents had died when she was a little girl. She had been raised by her cousin Mordecai. Mordecai knew that Esther was indeed beautiful.

Ahasuerus chose Esther as the new queen of Persia. Mordecai saw very little of Esther after that, but he did send her messages.

One day Mordecai heard two men plotting to kill the king. He sent word to Esther. Mordecai had saved the life of King Ahasuerus. The king never knew that Mordecai the Jew was his wife's relative.

1. *How did Ahasuerus find a new queen?*
2. *How did Mordecai save the king's life?*

Haman Plans to Kill Jews

Esther 3:1-5:8

King Ahasuerus let a man named Haman run much of the empire. The king even required everyone to bow to Haman when he passed. Mordecai was the only one who refused to bow. Mordecai would bow only in prayer to God. Haman was furious that Mordecai refused too obey him.

Haman plotted to destroy all of the Jews in the kingdom. No one knew that Esther was a Jew.

Haman went to the king. He told the king his plan to destroy all Jews, women and children included. The king did not care. He gave him permission to do as he pleased.

Haman put out the order to destroy all Jews on the thirteenth day of the twelfth month.

Mordecai was sad. He sent a copy of the order to Esther with a servant. He told the servant to pass on this message. "Tell Esther to go to the king and plead for her people." Mordecai also warned Esther that she might be killed, too.

Esther had a plan. She told Mordecai to gather all of the Jews in Shusan. They were to pray for her for three days. She said, "If I die, I die."

Esther then went to the king. She asked that Ahasuerus and Haman have dinner with her. They promised to come.

1. *What did Haman plan to do to the Jews?*
2. *What was Esther's secret?*

Esther's Dinner

Esther 5:9-10:3

O n the third day Esther put on her royal
robes and walked into the king's hall.
The king called to her. He told her that
she could have whatever she requested. She
asked that Haman be brought in for the
banquet. The king sent for Haman. Again the
king asked for her request.

She asked that the three meet again for
another banquet the next night.

Haman was excited about the dinner with
the king and queen. He boasted to his wife.

He was still upset that Mordecai would not
bow down to him. He was ready for Mordecai
to die.

That night King Ahasuerus could not sleep.
He decided to read the history of the empire.
He learned that Mordecai had save his life.

The next day he asked Haman the best way to honor a man. Haman thought he was the man the king wanted to honor. He said, "Give him a royal robe and a royal horse. Let him ride through the city with a nobleman shouting, "this is what is done for a man honored by the king!" The king was happy with the idea. He told Haman to do this for the Jew Mordecai. Haman was mad.

Soon the king and Haman went into Esther's banquet. While they were eating she asked, "Let my life and the lives of my people be spared. They have been sold and will be destroyed." "Who should do such a thing?" said the king. "The enemy is the wicked Haman," said Esther.

The king saved Esther and her people. Haman was hanged. To this day, the Jewish people celebrate a special festival called Purim. They tell the story of Esther and Mordecai.

1. *What was Esther's request to the king?*
2. *What is the festival called Purim?*

The Trials of Job

Job 1:1-42:17

There was a rich man named Job who lived near Canaan. He was a very good man.

One day Satan spoke to God. God told Satan there was no one as loyal as Job. Job rejects all evil.

Satan challenged God. "Take away all that he had and he will hate you." God told Satan to do what he wanted with Job.

Soon Job saw trouble. In one day his animals were driven away. His children were killed and his house fell in. Job said, "God gave me everything. He can take it away. I came into the world with nothing, and I can leave with nothing."

God told Satan that Job was still full of right. Satan said, "Let me make him sick and we will see how good he will be." God told Satan he still trusted Job.

Satan brought painful sores to Job's body, but still he would not speak bad of God. Job's wife and friends all questioned why Job was still faithful. His friends thought he did something to anger God.

God then told everyone that Job spoke the truth. He knew God's goodness and never failed to trust him. Job prayed for his friends. God returned to Job twice as much as he had lost.

1. *What did Job do when he lost everything?*
2. *How did God repay Job for his loyalty?*

Daniel

Daniel 6:1-28

When the Persians took over Babylon one of those captured was a prophet named Daniel. Daniel had lived in Babylon since the days of King Nebuchadnezzar. Daruis was appointed the king of Babylon by the Persians.

Daniel was made one of three presidents in the land. The other two presidents were jealous of Daniel. They decided to plot against him. Everyone knew that Daniel prayed three times each day. He prayed toward Jerusalem.

The two presidents went to King Darius. They told him that since he was king, the people should pray to him. They wrote a new law declaring that everyone would pray to the king. If they did not, they would be thrown to the lions. Darius signed the law.

Daniel continued praying to his God. King Darius liked Daniel. Daniel's enemies made the king uphold the new law. King Darius was forced to throw Daniel to the lions. He told Daniel, "You are a faithful servant to your God. I hope He will save you from the lions."

King Darius worried all night about Daniel. The next morning he ran to the lions' den. The king did not think Daniel would be alive. He yelled into the den, "Did your God keep you safe?" To his surprise Daniel answered him. "God knew I had done nothing wrong," said Daniel. King Darius punished the men who were jealous of Daniel.

1. *Why did the men convince the king to pass the new law?*
2. *Who saved Daniel from the lions?*

Jonah and the Fish

Jonah 1:1-2:10

Assyria was a nation that was gaining power. Its capital was Nineveh, a large city enclosed in walls. Israel was in danger of falling under the power of Assyria. The Lord talked to the prophet Jonah. The Lord told Jonah to go to Nineveh and preach the word. The people of Nineveh needed to be saved from their wickedness.

But Jonah ran away from the Lord. He went to Joppa, found a ship bound for Tarshish, and paid the fare to take him away. The Lord sent a violent storm that threatened to break up the ship in the water. The sailors were afraid. Each sailor prayed to his god.

Jonah went below deck and fell asleep. The captain of the ship found him. He told Jonah to pray to his God to save them all. The sailors cast lots to find out the person responsible for the storm. The lot was cast on Jonah. He told the sailors that he was responsible because he had fled his Lord. The Lord who had made the sea and the land.

The sea was getting rougher. Jonah told the sailors that if they threw him into the water the sea would become calm. They tried instead to continue rowing, but the storm grew stronger.

Finally the sailors said a prayer asking for forgiveness, then threw Jonah into the sea. The water became very calm.

The Lord sent a large fish to swallow Jonah. He was inside the fish for three days and nights. While inside the fish he prayed to the Lord. The fish spit Jonah onto dry land.

1. *Why did the ship Jonah was on run into a storm?*
2. *How did God save Jonah?*

Jonah in Nineveh

Jonah 3:1-4:11

Upon entering the city of Nineveh, Jonah told the people, "Nineveh will be destroyed within forty days because it is so wicked!" He preached all over the city telling all that they would suffer because of the wickedness. They had sinned against God.

The people had never seen a prophet of God before. They stopped in the streets to listen to him. Some ran to tell their king what Jonah was saying. Even the king was frightened. He took off his rich clothes and dressed in sackcloth. He sat in ashes to show he was sorry for his sins. He told all of the citizens of Nineveh to ask for mercy from God.

Jonah finished his preaching and left the city walls. He waited for the fire. He hoped this Assyrian city, an enemy of Israel, would be destroyed.

Jonah waited past the forty days. God spared Nineveh because the people believed Jonah's message. They repented for their sins. Jonah was so unhappy he prayed to die.

God sent a vine to grow over Jonah's head to shade him from the burning sun. The next night a worm chewed on the vine until it withered and died. Again Jonah wished he were dead.

God said to Jonah, "You were concerned about the vine even though you did not make it grow. Shouldn't you feel more sorry for the people of Nineveh than you do for a vine?"

Jonah finally understood that God loved all people.

1. *How did the people of Nineveh react to Jonah's preaching?*
2. *What lesson was God trying to teach Jonah?*

Zechariah's Vision

Luke 1:1-23

The story of the New Testament started while Herod was king of Israel or Judea for the Roman Empire. Rome was ruled by Caesar Augustus.

Herod had rebuilt the Jewish temple. An old priest named Zechariah helped in the temple. Zechariah and his wife Elizabeth had never had children because Elizabeth was barren. One day it was Zechariah's turn to go to the temple and burn incense. The worshippers were praying outside. He was alone in the temple when an angel came to him.

"Do not be afraid, Zechariah, your prayer has been heard. You and Elizabeth will have a son you will name John. He will bring many of the people of Israel back to God."

Zechariah asked the angel, "How can I be sure of what you are saying? Elizabeth and I are very old."

The angel answered, "I am Gabriel. I speak for God. Because you question God, you will not speak until this event occurs."

When Zechariah stepped out of the temple the people realized he had seen a vision. He tried to tell them what had happened, but he was unable to speak. He returned home to wait.

1. *What promise did the angel make to Zechariah?*
2. *Why couldn't Zechariah speak when he came out of the temple?*

Gabriel Visits Mary

Luke 1:26-38

God sent the angel Gabriel to Nazareth, a town in Galilee, to a young virgin named Mary. She was pledged to marry Joseph, a descendant of David. The angel said, "Greetings! The Lord is with you."

Mary was frightened, but the angel continued, "Do not be afraid. You have found favor with God and will give birth to a son. You are to name him Jesus. He will be great. God will give him the throne of David, and He will reign over the house of Jacob forever."

Mary was confused. She could not see how this could happen because she was still a virgin. The angel answered, "The Holy Spirit will come to you. Your child will be the Son of God. Even your relative Elizabeth will have a child in her old age. Nothing is impossible with God."

Mary said, "I will serve the Lord as you have said." Then the angel Gabriel left her.

1. *What did Gabriel tell Mary?*
2. *What did she promise to do for the Lord?*

The Birth of John the Baptist

Luke 1:57-80

When it was time for Elizabeth to have her baby, she gave birth to a son. Her friends, neighbors, and relatives all shared her joy. They felt God had shown her mercy by giving her this special child.

As was tradition on the eighth day the child was to be circumcised. All present wanted to name him Zechariah, but Elizabeth spoke up and said, "No, he is to be named John." Everyone questioned her because there was no one in her family named John. Everyone wondered why he would not be named for his father.

They all looked at Zechariah. Zechariah asked for a writing tablet. He wrote on the tablet, "his name shall be John." Immediately Zechariah could speak again for the first time since the angel had appeared to him. He sang a song of thanks to God. He praised God and blessed him.

The neighbors and friends were astonished. They realized the Lord was with this child and wondered what future the Lord had for him.

The child grew and became strong in spirit. He stayed in the desert until it was time for him to preach. He was the great prophet John the Baptist.

1. *When could Zechariah speak again?*
2. *Why did the neighbors and friends think this child would be blessed?*

The Birth of Jesus

Matthew 1:18-21 and Luke 2:1-7

Caesar Augustus issued a decree that a census would be taken of all who lived in the Roman world. Everyone was told to go to their hometown to be counted. Joseph left Nazareth in Galilee to go to Bethlehem in Judea because he belonged to the house of David. He took Mary with him because they were betrothed. Mary was expecting a baby.

An angel had visited Joseph, a carpenter, and told him the child Mary carried belonged to the Holy Spirit. The angel told Joseph the child would be a boy, and he and Mary were to name the child Jesus. The child would save people from their sins.

The town was crowded with people who came to be counted. There was no room for Mary and Joseph in the inn, so they stayed in the stable with the animals. That night while they were in the stable, Mary had her baby. She wrapped the child in a blanket and placed him in a manger which was used to place feed for the animals.

1. Why did Joseph and Mary travel to Bethlehem?
2. Where did Mary have her baby?

The Shepherds and the Angels

Luke 2:8-20

There were shepherds who lived nearby. They guarded their sheep day and night. While watching their sheep one night a bright light glowed above them. There was an angel in the light. The shepherds were afraid.

But the angel said, "Don't be afraid. I bring good news. There will be a great joy to all people. Today is born in the city of David a Savior. He is the Christ. Go and find him wrapped in a blanket and lying in a manger."

Suddenly there were a large number of angels who appeared. They were praising God and saying, "Glory to God in the highest, and peace to all people on earth."

After the angels left, the shepherds talked for a while. One finally said, "Let's go to Bethlehem and see this child described by the angels."

They hurried to town and searched until they found Mary and Joseph and the baby. They told everyone they saw about the angels' visit and the birth of the child. All who heard were amazed. The shepherds glorified and praised God for what they had heard and seen. They felt blessed to be a part of this birth.

Mary thought over all of the things that were said. She said nothing, but kept them in her heart.

1. *What did the shepherds see?*
2. *Who did the shepherds visit?*

The Star and the Wise Men

Matthew 2:1-12

Shortly after Jesus was born, Magi or Wise Men came from the east to Jerusalem asking, "Where is the child who was born King of the Jews? We have seen his star, and we came to worship him?"

King Herod was afraid he would lose his kingdom to this new "king." He ordered that priests and scribes find out where this child was born. The Jewish priests explained that the prophet Micah predicted the child would be born in Bethlehem.

Herod spoke untruthfully to the Wise Men. He told them to tell him when they found the child so he could honor him.

The Wise Men continued their journey and their search for the child. They stopped over the place where they saw the star. There they found the child. They were excited and thrilled. They bowed down and worshiped him.

They presented the child with gifts of gold, incense, and myrrh, a resin from a shrub used to make perfume or medicine.

The men were warned in a dream to return to their own country by a new route. They were warned against seeing Herod again.

1. *What were the Wise Men looking for?*
2. *Why did they not go back to tell Herod where the child was?*

Presenting the Baby in the Temple

Luke 2:21-40

As was the custom the child was taken to the temple on the eighth day to be circumcised. It also was custom for every firstborn male to be dedicated to the Lord. The name of the child would be Jesus which means "salvation." Mary and Joseph took Jesus to Jerusalem to fulfill this custom.

In the temple was a man named Simeon. He was a devout, old man. He had been told by God that he would live long enough to see the Christ. When Mary and Joseph entered with the child, Simeon took Jesus in his arms. He praised God saying, "He is a light to give light to the nations, and the glory of thy people Israel."

Mary and Joseph were amazed. Simeon told the parents, "Many in Israel will rise and fall because of Jesus."

When Mary and Joseph had done everything required by the Law, they returned home. Jesus grew and became strong. He was filled with wisdom, and God was always with him.

1. *What promise had God given Simeon?*
2. *What did Simeon say about Jesus?*

Escaping to Egypt

Matthew 2:13-23

An angel of the Lord appeared to Joseph. "Escape immediately with the child and his mother to Egypt. Stay there until I tell you it is safe. Herod is searching for the child because he wants to kill him."

Joseph left that night with Mary and Jesus. This fulfilled what the Lord had said through the prophet: "Out of Egypt I will call my son."

Herod was very angry when he realized the Wise Men fooled him. He gave orders to kill all of the boys in Bethlehem. Any boy under the age of two was to be killed.

When Herod died an angel told Joseph to go back to Israel. When he found out that Herod's son was ruling in Judea, he was afraid to go there. He was told in a dream to go to Galilee. Joseph took Mary and Jesus to Nazareth in Galilee. Again a prophet's words were fulfilled: "He will be called a Nazarene."

1. *Why did Herod decide to kill all boys?*
2. *Why did Joseph take Jesus to Nazareth to live?*

Jesus in the Temple

Luke 2:41-52

By the time Jesus was three years old he was living in Nazareth. He stayed there until he was about thirty years old.

When he was twelve years old, his family went to Jerusalem for the Feast of the Passover. After the Feast, his parents returned home, but Jesus stayed behind in Jerusalem. His parents thought he was with their group. They traveled for a day before they realized he was not with their relatives and friends. They returned to Jerusalem to look for him.

After three days they found him in the temple, sitting among the teachers, listening to them and asking questions.

Everyone who heard him was amazed that he understood what was being discussed. His mother said to him, "Why did you not come with us? Did you not realize we were worried about you?"

But Jesus answered, "Did you not know that I had to be in my Father's house?" They did not understand what he was saying.

He returned to Nazareth with his mother and Joseph. Mary watched Jesus grow in wisdom. He was truly in favor with God and men.

1. *Why did Jesus and his family go to Jerusalem?*
2. *What did Jesus do in the temple?*

John the Baptist

Luke 3:1-11

By the time John the Baptist, the son of Zechariah, was thirty years old, he was preaching the word of God in the desert. He went to all of the country around the Jordan. He told the people if they turned from their sins they would be forgiven. John baptized those who turned from sin in the Jordan river.

It was written by Isaiah the prophet:
A voice will call out of the desert,
He will be ahead of the Lord and
He will prepare a path for him.
Everyone will see God's salvation.

The crowds gathered when John spoke. John was a man whose words were different than what the people had been taught. He taught that everyone should share with a neighbor. He told them the kingdom of Heaven was nearby. The King would soon be present.

When the people asked what they should do, John told them, "If you have two coats, give one to someone who has none. If you have extra food, share it with someone who is hungry."

1. *What did John the Baptist preach?*
2. *What did he do for the people when they turned from sin?*

The Baptism of Jesus

Luke 3:21-23; Matthew 3:13-17; John 1:31-34

When Jesus was about thirty years old, he began his ministry. He traveled from Galilee to the Jordan River to be baptized by John.

The crowd wondered if John the Baptist was the Christ. He told the people another would come who was greater than any other man. John was in the river when Jesus arrived. Jesus came to be baptized by John. When John saw Jesus, he realized he was holier than himself. John said, "You come to me? You should baptize me." Jesus said, "It is proper and right that you should do this, John."

John baptized Jesus as he had others. When Jesus came out of the water he was praying. John saw the heavens open up. He saw the Spirit of God appear as a dove. Lightening appeared. A voice from Heaven said, "This is my Son. I love him and I am pleased with him." John told the crowd of people that this was the Son of God.

1. *Who came to John to be baptized?*
2. *What did God say about Jesus?*

Satan Tempts Jesus

Matthew 4:1-11; Luke 4:1-13

After his baptism the Spirit of God led Jesus into the wilderness where he was tempted by Satan. He fasted for forty days and nights and was then very hungry. Satan said, "If you are the Son of God, turn these stones into bread."

Jesus answered, "It is written: man does not live by bread alone. He lives on the word that comes from God."

The devil took him to the holy city and had him stand at the highest point of the temple. "If you are the Son of God, jump and you won't get hurt." Jesus answered, "It is written: Do not put God to a test."

Next, the devil took Jesus to a very high mountain. "I will give you everything you can see if you will bow down and worship me."

Jesus replied, "Get away from me, Satan! For it is written: Worship and serve only God!"

1. *What was Satan trying to do to Jesus?*
2. *What does Jesus say is food besides bread?*

Jesus Chooses the First Disciples

Matthew 4:18-22; Mark 1:16-20; Luke 5:2-11

After his victory over Satan, Jesus returned to the Sea of Galilee. A crowd immediately gathered around Jesus as he was walking. At the edge of the water he saw two boats left there by fishermen. Two brothers were washing their nets. One was Simon (whom Jesus later called Peter) and the other was Andrew. He got into one of the boats and pushed out a little from the shore. He sat down in the boat and taught the people.

Peter and Andrew listened to what Jesus was saying. Then Jesus said to them, "Come follow me and I will make you fishers of men." The brothers dropped their nets and followed him.

As they continued to walk, they saw two other brothers, James and John. They were the sons of Zebedee. They, too, were in a boat preparing nets. Jesus called to them and they left the boat and their father and followed Jesus.

1. *What did Peter and Andrew do for a living?*
2. *What did Jesus tell them would happen if they followed him?*

Jesus, Disciples and the First Miracle

John 1:43-2:11

The next day Jesus had more disciples join him as he preached. Philip was from the same town as Andrew and Peter. Philip found Nathanael and told him, "We have found the man Moses wrote about. He is Jesus of Nazareth."

When Nathanael saw him he said, "Teacher, you are the Son of God." Jesus said, "You shall see great things. You shall see the Heaven open before you and the angels of God shall appear."

Three days later a wedding took place. Jesus' mother came to him and said, "They are out of wine." Jesus replied, "Dear woman, why tell me? My time has not yet come."

But nearby stood six water jugs. Each jug held 20 to 30 gallons. Jesus told the servants to fill the jars with water. They did so. Then the servants took the jugs to the owner of the home where the wedding was held. He tasted the wine and told the bridegroom this wine tasted better than what was served first.

Jesus performed this first miracle at Cana in Galilee. There were now six followers called disciples. The word disciples means "learner." The disciples put their faith in him.

1. *Who did Nathanael say Jesus was?*
2. *What miracle did Jesus perform at the wedding?*

Clearing the Temple

John 2:12-22

Jesus went to Capernaum with his mother and younger brothers. After a few days Jesus went to Jerusalem for it was time for the Jewish Passover. This was the feast held every year to remind people how God had led them out of Egypt many years ago.

In the temple Jesus found men selling sheep and doves for sacrifices. Other men were at tables changing money for the Jews who came from other lands into the money of Judea. Jesus looked around and became very angry. He made a whip out of cords. He drove the animals away, and he scattered the money of the money changers and turned over their tables. He shouted, "How dare you turn my Father's house into a market!"

The Jews were angry. "Why do you think you have authority to do this?"

Jesus told them to destroy the temple. He would raise it up in three days. But Jesus was not talking about the building. The temple he spoke of was his body. They would put him to death, but he would come back in three days.

After he was raised from the dead, the disciples remembered what he had said.

1. *What did Jesus go to the temple to celebrate?*
2. *Why was he angry with those in the temple?*

Nicodemus Visits at Night

John 3:1-21

Nicodemus was a Pharisee, a member of the Jewish council. The Pharisees strongly opposed Jesus. This was why Nicodemus met with Jesus at night. It was too dangerous for him to meet with Jesus in public.

Nicodemus told Jesus, "We know you are a teacher who has come from God. No one can perform miracles unless God is with him."

Jesus replied, "The truth is, no one can see God's kingdom until he is born again of the Spirit." Nicodemus was confused. "How can a person be born a second time?"

You are a teacher of Israel and you do not understand these things?" remarked Jesus. "Moses lifted up the brass serpent on a pole and whoever saw it escaped the poison of the snakes." Finally Nicodemus understood.

Jesus continued. "I will be on the cross and whoever believes in me shall have all sin removed. God loved the world so much that He gave His only Son. Whoever believes in Him will not die, but will have eternal life."

1. *Why did Nicodemus meet with Jesus at night?*
2. *What promise did Jesus make Nicodemus about being born again?*

The Woman at the Well

John 4:6-30

While traveling through Samaria Jesus and his followers came to rest by Jacob's well about noontime. His followers left Jesus at the well while they went to buy food. Tired from the journey, Jesus sat down by the well.

When a Samaritan woman came up to the well to draw water, Jesus asked her for a drink. "You know that Jews don't share with Samaritans," she said.

Jesus smiled. "If you knew who was asking for a drink, you would be asking me for one. I would give you living water."

"You don't even have a bucket," the woman said. "How will you get your living water?" Jesus told the woman, "The water in this well will make you thirsty again, but the water from the well inside of you is a spring that provides eternal life."

The woman knew Jesus was a prophet. She asked if she should worship at the mountain or worship at Jerusalem. Jesus continued to talk to her. "You no longer need to worship in either place. God wants all people to worship in spirit and in truth. God is Spirit."

"I know the Messiah will come soon. When he does, he will explain all of this to us," she said. Jesus looked at the woman. "It is the Christ who is speaking to you."

Soon Jesus' followers returned with food. They were surprised to see Jesus talking with the Samaritan woman. The woman dropped her water jug and ran back to town. She told everyone to come listen to the man at the well.

Because of the woman, the people came out of the town to look for Jesus. Many listened and believed what Jesus said.

1. *Why was the woman surprised that Jesus spoke to her?*
2. *What kind of water does Jesus give?*

Healing the Official's Son

John 4:43-54

Jesus left for Galilee. The Galileans welcomed him. Many people had been following him from place to place, so word of his deeds was spreading. They had seen what he had done at the Passover Feast in Jerusalem. Some had seen him turn water into wine in Cana.

Now there was an official whose son was sick at Capernaum. The man traveled to Galilee to beg him to heal his son, who was close to death.

Jesus told him, "Unless you see miracles, you will not believe." "Please come down before my son dies," the nobleman begged. "Go now," Jesus said, "for your son will live."

The man believed Jesus and left for home. While he was still on the way home, a servant met him with news that his son was living. He asked when his son had started to get better. The servant told him the fever left him yesterday at the seventh hour. The father realized that was the exact time he was talking to Jesus. All of his household believed from that time forward.

This was the second time Jesus performed a miracle to prove he was the Son of God.

1. *Why did the official go to Jesus for help?*
2. *What did Jesus do for the man?*

Jesus in Nazareth

Luke 4:14-24

Jesus returned to Galilee with the Spirit. News about him spread through the countryside. He taught in the synagogues. Then he went to Nazareth, his home. As was his custom he went to the synagogue on the Sabbath day. The scroll of the prophet Isaiah was handed to him to read.

The Spirit of the Lord is on me,
Because he has anointed me
To preach good news to the poor.
He has sent me to give freedom to
prisoners,
And recover sight for the blind,
And to release the oppressed.
It is the year of God's grace to all people.

He rolled up the scroll and gave it back to the attendant and sat down. He said, "Today you have heard the scripture come true." Everyone was amazed at his gracious words. One asked, "Isn't this Joseph's son? How can he teach us?"

Jesus said to them, "You will say, why isn't he doing here what he did in Capernaum? The truth is, a prophet is never welcome in his hometown."

1. *Why did the people come to see Jesus in Nazareth?*
2. *Why then did the people question Jesus?*

Jesus Is Rejected

Luke 4:24-31

The people in the synagogue began to whisper. No one believed a carpenter could teach them. "This man is no teacher. He is just the son of Joseph!" "If he can perform miracles in other places, why can't he perform them here?" "Show us some miracles!"

"I know you all want to see a miracle like the one on the official's son," Jesus said, "but no prophet is ever welcome in his own hometown."

Jesus gave examples of Elijah's time. The only leper Elijah healed was from Syria. When no rain came, God told Elijah to help a woman who was not a Jew.

Everyone in the synagogue was furious. They wanted miracles, too. They drove Jesus out of town to the highest hill. They wanted to throw him off a cliff. Jesus slipped away from the crowd.

The next day he went to Capernaum, a town in Galilee, and taught the people on the Sabbath. They were amazed at his words and teachings. Unlike other teachers, Jesus spoke with authority and knowledge.

1. *Name an example that shows prophets are not welcome in their own town.*
2. *Why were the people angry at Jesus?*

Driving Out an Evil Spirit

Luke 4:33-44

In the synagogue in Capernaum there was a man with an evil spirit. He yelled to Jesus, "What do you want with us, Jesus of Nazareth? Leave us alone. I know you are the Holy One of God!"

"Come out of him now!" Jesus said with firmness in his voice. The demon threw the man to the ground and came out without hurting him.

The people stood watching in amazement. "He gives orders and an evil spirit leaves a man's body!" The news was spread throughout the area.

Jesus left the synagogue and went home with Simon. Simon's mother-in-law was sick with a high fever. The family asked Jesus for help. He bent over her and condemned the fever. The fever immediately left the woman, and she got up and began to help get them a meal.

By sunset the news had spread. People with all types of sickness were brought to Jesus. He laid his hands on each one and healed them.

At daybreak Jesus went to a quiet place to pray. The people followed him because they did not want him to leave. But Jesus said, "I must preach the good news of the kingdom of God to other towns. That is why I was sent." And so he continued on to preach in other synagogues.

1. *What was wrong with Simon's mother-in-law?*
2. *What did Jesus tell the people when they wanted him to stay?*

Jesus Calls Matthew

Matthew 9:9-13; Mark 2:14-17; Luke 5:27-32

There lived one group of Jews who were hated. They were tax collectors who worked for the Roman government. The Jews wanted to be an independent nation with their own ruler. They didn't like the Romans or any one who worked for the Romans.

It was well known that some of the tax collectors took more money than the government charged. They stole from the people to become rich themselves. Because of this, people thought all tax collectors were dishonest.

One day Jesus was walking along a street in Capernaum. He saw Matthew collecting tax money from people. Jesus knew that in his heart Matthew was a good man. He went up to Matthew and said, "Follow me. Be my disciple."

With gladness in his heart, Matthew left the money table and followed Jesus. He also wanted his friends to hear the words of Jesus.

Matthew gave a great banquet, and he invited many of his friends. Some were tax collectors. Jesus and all of his disciples attended the banquet.

Even though they were not invited, many scribes and Pharisees gathered in the courtyard around Matthew's house. They whispered about the party. They criticized Jesus for being with these sinners.

Finally the scribes and Pharisees called to Jesus' disciples and asked, "Why does your Master eat and drink with the tax collectors and sinners?"

Jesus heard what these proud Jews had said. He answered, "Those who are well do not need a doctor. The doctor sees the people who are sick. I have come to call on sinners to repent."

Many of the tax collectors and sinners asked for forgiveness of their sins. Matthew became another of Jesus' disciples.

1. *What did the scribes and Pharisees ask the disciples?*
2. *Who did Jesus say needed to hear the Word?*

Healing the Cripple at the Pool

John 5:1-18

Jesus went to Jerusalem for the Passover Feast. There was a pool called Bethesda. Many disabled people visited there each year to bathe in the waters. When Jesus arrived there was a man there who had been an invalid for 38 years. Jesus asked him if he wanted to get well.

"I have no one to help me get in the waters. Every time I try, someone always goes ahead of me."

Jesus said to the man, "Get up now. Take your mat and walk." The man was immediately cured. He picked up his mat and walked away.

This event took place on the Sabbath. The Jews told the man he should not be carrying his mat on the Sabbath. The man said, "The man who cured me told me to pick up my mat and walk." They questioned him. They wanted to know who would tell him such a thing. The man did not know who Jesus was.

The man later saw Jesus in the temple. He pointed Jesus out to the men. The Jews persecuted Jesus for doing these things on the Sabbath.

"My Father works every day, so I will work every day, also."

This made the Jews mad for not only was Jesus working on the Sabbath but he was making himself equal to God."

1. *Why was the disabled man at the pool in Bethesda?*
2. *Why were the Jews upset with Jesus?*

Jesus Heals on the Sabbath

Matthew 12:1-15; Mark 3:1-6; Luke 6:1-11

After Jesus angered the Pharisees by healing the disabled man on the Sabbath, they became his enemies. Many followed wherever Jesus went.

On another Sabbath Jesus and his disciples walked through a grainfield. The disciples were hungry so they picked some grain, rubbed them in their hands, and ate the kernels. Some of the Pharisees saw this and asked, "Why are you allowing your disciples to gather food to eat on the Sabbath?"

Jesus answered, "Have you never heard what David did when his men where hungry? He entered the tabernacle and took the consecrated bread. He ate what was there for the priests, then he shared the rest with his men. The Son of man is lord of the Sabbath."

Jesus then went to the synagogue to teach. There he saw a man with a withered hand. The Pharisees were still watching him closely. They actually tried to think of questions that would trick Jesus.

"Is it unlawful to heal on the Sabbath?" one asked of Jesus. Jesus answered, "If you have a sheep to fall into a pit on the Sabbath, would you not get it out? Isn't a man more valuable than a sheep?" The Pharisees said no more, but they were angry.

Jesus called to the man with the withered hand, "Stretch out your hand." The man obeyed and immediately his hand was healed. The Pharisees were so mad they left the synagogue so they could plan a way to kill Jesus.

Jesus knew what the Pharisees were planning. He continued to have large crowds follow him, and he continued to heal all of the sick among them.

1. *What did the disciples do on the Sabbath?*
2. *Why did the Pharisees question Jesus' actions on the Sabbath?*

The Twelve Disciples

Matthew 10:1-4; Mark 3:13-19; Luke 6:12-16

By now Jesus had many followers including, the four fishermen, Phillip, Nathanael, and Matthew. Many people followed Jesus from place to place. Many wanted to be his pupils.

Jesus felt it was time to choose the twelve who would receive special training to help him with his work. He would send these men to places he had never been. They would preach to all they could about the kingdom of God.

Jesus wanted God's help in choosing this special twelve. One night he quietly climbed a mountain to pray. He prayed all night for wisdom and strength. He prayed for God to help him do his work. When morning came he joined his followers in the valley. He was ready to choose his helpers.

From those with him he chose Simon, whom he called Peter, and Andrew, the brothers. Then he chose James and John, the brothers who had been partners with Simon and Andrew in the fishing business. Next he chose Matthew, the tax collector; Philip, of Bethesda; Thomas and Bartholomew, also called Nathanael; James the Less, the son of Alphaeus; another Simon who was called a zealot; Thaddeus; and last of all Judas Iscariot.

Jesus trained these twelve to preach the kingdom of God. He gave them the power to heal. He called them apostles which means, "those who are sent out."

1. *What does apostle mean?*
2. *Name as many of the disciples or apostles as you remember.*

The Sermon on the Mount

Matthew 5:1-9 and Luke 6: 17-22

Jesus wanted to teach his disciples how to do his work. He climbed up the mountainside and sat down. Huge crowds followed Jesus and the disciples up the mountain. All came to listen to Jesus teach.

> Blessed are the poor in spirit, for theirs is the kingdom of Heaven.
>
> Blessed are the meek, for they will inherit the earth.
>
> Blessed are those who are hungry, for they shall be filled.
>
> Blessed are the merciful, for they will be shown mercy.
>
> Blessed are the pure in heart, for they will see God.
>
> Blessed are the peacemakers, for they shall be called the children of God.

In this sermon Jesus teaches all how God loves and cares for them. He taught how to pray and how to love friends and enemies.

1. *Who listened to the sermon on the mount?*
2. *Who are the children of God?*

The Faith of the Centurion

Luke 7:1-10

Jesus returned to Capernaum. News of his arrival spread quickly. Here lived an officer of the Roman army. He was called a centurion because he was the leader of 100 men. He had a favorite servant who was near death. The centurion sent someone to ask Jesus if he could heal his servant.

The people told Jesus that he was a worthy man. He paid to have a synagogue built. Jesus started to the man's house.

Not far from the centurion's house Jesus encountered some of the friends of the centurion. They brought a message from him. "Lord, I don't deserve to have you in my house. You are a great man. I know that you can speak the words that will heal my servant. Like you, I have someone who tells me what to do then I give orders to my soldiers."

Jesus was amazed at his words. Jesus spoke to the crowd who had gathered hoping to see another miracle. "Nowhere among the Jews have I found someone who has this kind of faith in me."

When the friends returned to the house, they found the servant healed.

1. *Why did the centurion deserve Jesus' help?*
2. *What did Jesus say about his faith?*

Men on the Roof

Matthew 9:2-8 and Luke 5:18-26

By now crowds followed Jesus wherever he went. They gathered in the streets. They gathered at the houses where he stayed. Some were friends and believers. Some were just curious. Others enjoyed finding fault in what he said.

One day in Capernaum Jesus was preaching about the kingdom of God to his disciples and friends. He was in a house. People continued to come until there was such a crowd not one more person could get in the house.

While Jesus was talking, they heard a strange noise above them. Soon the roof began to open. The people saw a man lying on a cot being lowered from the ceiling.

From the roof four friends of the crippled man watched. They asked Jesus to heal their friend. He could not move and was getting weaker each day. Because of the crowd the friends had not been able to get the man through the door of the house. That is why they lifted him to the roof.

He said, "Simon, let me tell you a story. A rich man loaned money to two poor men. He loaned $500 to one man and $50 to the other. Neither man could pay the man back. The rich man forgave them both. Which of these two men will love the rich man more?'

Simon thought carefully. "I suppose the man who owed the most."

"That is right," said Jesus. "When I came into your home, Simon, you did not treat me like an honored guest. You did not give me water to wash the dirt from my feet. But this woman washed my feet with her tears and dried them with her hair. You did not kiss me welcome. You did not anoint my head with oil as you do your friends. This woman poured perfume on my feet and kissed them. Her sins are forgiven for she has much love. The one who's done little to forgive, loves little.

Jesus told the woman, "Your sins are forgiven." The people around the table murmured, "Who is this who forgives sins?"

"Your faith has saved you," he said, "Go in peace."

1. *Who had more sins, Simon or the woman?*
2. *Which one showed more love for Jesus?*

The Parable of the Sower

Matthew 13:1-23; Mark 4:1-20; Luke 8:4-15

One day Jesus went to sit by the lake. Such large crowds gathered that he got in a boat and sat down in it. The people stayed on shore. Then he told them about parables, short stories that show truths of the gospels. Here is one story.

One day a farmer took a bag of grain out to his field. He walked back and forth spreading grain on the ground. There was a wind that day that helped spread the seeds.

Some seeds blew onto the road. Birds flew down and ate them. Other seeds fell in rocks. They died because there wasn't enough water. Seeds fell into the weeds and could not grow. Many of them fell on good soil. They sprouted and in time grew into stalks of grain. These gave the farmer a good crop.

The disciples were not sure of the meaning of the story so they asked Jesus. Jesus then told the disciples, "The farmer is the person who speaks the word of God. The different kinds of soil are the way people act when they hear the word of God. Some hear but do not try to understand like the roadside where the seeds fell. The birds came down and ate the seeds. In life the evil one comes and people forget the message.

"The seeds in the rocks are the people who believe for a little while. But in hard times, they forget God's word.

"The seeds in the weeds represent the people who hear God's word, but go on their way. They have things like trouble, money and pleasure in their heart. God can't get in.

"Then there are the seeds in the good soil. These are full of God's word. The life of the person who let's God in his or her heart is changed forever."

1. *What is a parable?*
2. *Tell what kinds of seeds fell.*

Jesus Calms the Water

Matthew 8:23-27; Mark 4:35-41; Luke 8:22-25

Jesus spent all day preaching and the crowds were so large they were pressing close to him. There was no room or time to rest. He asked his followers to row him across the Sea of Galilee. The disciples and Jesus went in one boat. Some who saw him leave got into their own small boats to follow.

While out in the middle of the water a huge storm came up. Large waves hit the boat. The disciples had no control over it. A great wave swept over the boat and flooded it with water. They were afraid it might sink. What should they do?

Jesus was so tired from teaching and preaching all day that he was asleep. The storm didn't bother him.

The disciples decided to wake Jesus because the boat was about to sink. "Master, we will die in the storm!"

Jesus opened his eyes and looked around. He saw many frightened faces. "Do you not have faith?" Jesus stood up and spoke to the wind and sea. "Peace, be still." The sea became calm when he spoke.

The disciples were amazed. "Even the wind and the sea obey him."

1. *Why were the disciples afraid?*
2. *What did Jesus say about their faith?*

Saving the Little Girl

Matthew 9:18-1-:42; Mark 5:22-42;
Luke 8:41-9:6

Jesus and his disciples again crossed the sea by boat to Capernaum. And again a crowd waited on the shore to welcome them.

A Jewish leader named Jairus came running toward Jesus and fell at his feet. "My precious daughter is about to die. Please come touch her so she will live." Jesus and the crowd followed him.

In the crowd was a woman who had been ill for twelve years. She had been to doctor after doctor, but no one could cure her. She tried hard to talk to Jesus, but she could barely get through the crowd. She finally was able to reach Jesus' clothes. When she touched his cloak, she was immediately healed.

Jesus knew what the woman had done. He turned around and asked, "Who touched me?" Many in the crowd had pushed toward him, but he had felt the healing power go from his body.

The trembling woman came forward and fell on her knees. Jesus touched her and said, "Your faith has made you well. Go in peace."

By this time someone had run up to Jairus and told him that his daughter was dead. It was too late for Jesus to help.

Jesus heard the messenger and looked at Jairus. "Have faith and she will be made well."

As they arrived at Jairus' home, they saw people weeping. "Why do you weep?" Jesus said, "She is just sleeping."

Jesus sent everyone out of the room except for the father and mother and Peter, James and John. He reached for the little girl's head. "Get up, my child." He told her mother, "Now feed her." He asked that they tell no one what he had done. His job was to heal souls, not raise the dead. The crowds were already too large.

Jesus then decided to send his twelve disciples to other cities. He sent them in pairs so they could help each other. He told them to preach the gospel and heal the sick. Jesus could no longer do his work alone.

1. *What happened when the woman touched Jesus?*
2. *What did Jesus do at Jairus' house?*

The Death of John the Baptist

Matthew 14:1-12; 11:7-15

King Herod was a mean man. He had married his brother's wife, Herodias. When John the Baptist heard of this he announced it was against the law. Herod put John in prison. Herod was afraid to do more to John because he knew him as a prophet.

A feast was held on Herod's birthday. Herodias' daughter danced for Herod. He so enjoyed her performance, he promised her anything she wanted.

After talking with her mother, she asked for John the Baptist's head on a platter. Herod was unhappy, but everyone had heard him make the promise. He sent guards to cut off John's head. He presented the plate to the girl who then gave it to her mother.

John's followers went to the prison, took his body for burial, and then went to follow Jesus. They told Jesus what had happened and he said, "He was more than a prophet. The prophet Malachi wrote about him. He was the messenger sent ahead to prepare the way. No one greater was ever born than John the Baptist."

1. *Why did Herodias want to hurt John the Baptist?*
2. *What did John the Baptist do for Jesus?*

Jesus Feeds the Crowd

Matthew 14:13-23; Mark 6:30-46; Luke 9:10-17; John 6:1-15

The disciples returned telling about all of the people they had taught and healed. People were coming from everywhere to hear and see Jesus. He no longer had time to sleep or eat. Jesus asked the disciples to go with him to a quiet place for rest.

They sailed to the other side of the sea and went to a place in the desert hoping to find some peace. Again the people had followed them across the sea. "They are like sheep who have no shepherd," he said.

People stayed with him from early morning to late in the evening. No one seemed to realize there was no food or shelter in the desert. The disciples wanted to send the people away.

Jesus answered, "We must feed them before we send them away." He turned to Phillip. "Where can we find bread to eat?" Phillip knew they could never find enough.

There was a small boy in the crowd who had brought a lunch basket. In it were five loaves of bread and two small fishes.

The boy heard Jesus and the disciples talking. He offered to give the food to Jesus. Jesus took the loaves and fishes, gave thanks, and broke the food into small pieces as he placed it in baskets. He handed the baskets to each disciple.

When the crowd had eaten all they wanted, the disciples gathered up the food that was left. There were twelve baskets full.

1. *What did the disciples want to do about feeding the huge crowd?*
2. *What did Jesus do?*

Jesus Walks On Water

Matthew 14:22-36

After feeding the crowds, Jesus needed time to pray. He sent the disciples back to the boat. He went up the mountain alone. By evening the boat was out in the sea. In the early morning Jesus came to them walking on the sea.

They all cried in fear for they thought it was a ghost. "Don't be afraid," said Jesus, "It is I." Peter asked if he could walk on the water. Jesus told him to come. Peter started to walk toward Jesus, but the wind begin to blow. Peter cried out, "Lord, save me!"

Jesus reached and caught him. "Why did you doubt, Peter. Why do you have so little faith?" The disciples worshiped him and said he must truly be the Son of God.

When the boat arrived on land, the sick again were brought to Jesus. Many just wanted to touch the edge of Jesus' cloak. All who did were healed.

1. *Why were the disciples frightened when they saw Jesus on the water?*
2. *Why did Peter begin to sink?*

The Faith of A Gentile

Matthew 15:21-28; Mark 7:24-30

While Jesus was traveling, he came to a place where Gentiles lived. Gentiles were people from another country or people who were not Jews. Even the Gentiles had heard about Jesus and his preaching.

A Gentile woman ran up to Jesus and begged him for help. She said her daughter was possessed by an evil spirit. At first Jesus paid no attention to the woman. The woman continued to follow him crying for help.

The disciples tried to send her away. They felt she was bothering Jesus, and she was not a Jew. She fell at Jesus' feet and worshiped him. His heart ached. He wanted to help her. "I am not sent to the Gentiles, but to the lost people of Israel. It is not fair to take the children's bread and throw it to the dogs."

The woman knew that some Jews called Gentiles "dogs." She did not mind being called this if it would save her daughter.

She told Jesus, "The dogs will eat the crumbs that fall from the children's table." Jesus was so pleased with the faith of the woman that he told her. "Go home, your daughter is well."

When she returned home her daughter was on her bed, free of the evil spirit.

1. *Who was Jesus sent to teach?*
2. *What lesson did Jesus teach the disciples in this story?*

The Blind Man Sees

Mark 8:22-26

Near Bethesda, a town by the Sea of Galilee, lived a blind man. He had heard about this man who healed all who were brought to him. The blind man wanted to see.

When the blind man was told that Jesus and his twelve disciples were in Bethesda, he asked friends to lead him to the place where he could find Jesus.

Jesus no longer wanted to attract crowds. He knew his time on earth was short. He needed this time to train his disciples. He needed time to be alone with them.

Friends of the blind man asked Jesus for help. Jesus took the man by the hand and led him outside of town. Jesus wanted to be alone with the man. He placed his hands on the man's eyes. "Do you see anything?" "I see people who look like walking trees," the man said.

Once again Jesus put his hands on the man's eyes. His eyes opened and his sight was restored. The man could see everything clearly.

Jesus told him to go straight home. He did not want him to go to the town. He wanted to be alone with his disciples.

1. *Why did Jesus help the man?*
2. *Why did he tell the man to go straight home?*

Peter Speaks Up

Matthew 16:13-28; Mark 8:27-31;
Luke 9:19-27

From Bethesda Jesus led the disciples to Caesarea Philippi. There he asked his disciples, "Who do people say that I am?"

"Some say you are the prophet Elijah. Some say you are John the Baptist risen from the dead. Others believe you are Jeremiah or another prophet from long ago."

Jesus asked, "Who do you think I am?" Boldly Peter spoke up. "You are the Christ, the Son of the living God."

Jesus rejoiced to hear his words. "Bless you, Peter," he said, "for you have learned this from my Father in Heaven. And Peter, on this rock I will build my church. The church will always be stronger than Hell. I will give to you the keys of the kingdom of Heaven."

He then warned the disciples not to tell anyone that he was the Christ. He told the disciples what would happen very soon. "I will go to Jerusalem. There I will be killed. Three days later, I will return from the dead. God has sent me so these things will happen."

1. *Who did Peter say Jesus was?*
2. *Why did God send Jesus to earth?*

The Transfiguration

Mark 9:2-10; Matthew 17:1-13

About a week later Jesus took Peter, James, and John to the mountaintop. The disciples were tired, and they fell asleep. Jesus prayed alone.

While they slept, a change came over their Master. His face shone like the sun. His clothing was whiter than anything on earth. Suddenly, Moses and Elijah appeared and spoke to Jesus. The three discussed Jesus' coming death.

The three were still talking when the disciples woke up. The disciples were amazed to see these men.

Peter asked, "Shall we pitch three tents? One to worship you, one to worship Moses, and one for Elijah?" While Peter spoke, a cloud covered the disciples and they were afraid.

A voice came out of the cloud. "This is my beloved Son. I am pleased with him. Listen to what he says."

The disciples fell to the ground, trembling with fear. When they looked up, they saw only Jesus.

1. *Who was present with Jesus?*
2. *What did God tell the disciples?*

Healing the Little Boy

Matthew 17:14-21; Mark 9:14-29;
Luke 9:37-43

Jesus and the three disciples left the mountaintop and joined the other disciples who were surrounded by a crowd.

A man ran out of the crowd and fell at Jesus' feet. "Lord, have mercy on my son. He suffers terribly. Sometimes he falls into the fire. Sometimes he falls into the water. Your disciples could not cure him."

Jesus said, "Why do you continue to have no faith?" The boy was brought to Jesus. He demanded that the evil spirit come out. The boy stood up and walked to his father. He was completely well.

The disciples asked to speak to Jesus alone. "Why could we not do that?" they asked. "Because you have so little faith. Faith the size of a mustard seed can move a mountain. With faith, nothing is impossible." He continued to talk to them about their need for faith in God.

1. Why could the disciples not cure the boy?
2. What did Jesus tell the disciples they must have?

Forgiveness

Matthew 18:21-35

Peter asked Jesus, "How often should I forgive someone? Seven times?" Jesus answered, "Not seven times, but seventy times seven."

Peter wondered if he could ever forgive someone that many times. Jesus told a story.

Once a king's servant owed him a lot of money. He couldn't pay. The king ordered that the man and his family be sold into slavery to pay his debt.

The servant fell before him. "Have patience with me and I will pay all that I owe you!"

The king felt sorry for the man. He forgave the man his debt.

Later the servant saw a poor man who had borrowed a few dollars from him. He had the poor man put in jail because he could not pay. The king heard what had happened. "I forgave your large debt and had mercy on you. You should have had mercy on the poor man instead of sending him to prison."

Jesus told Peter, "My Father is like the king in this story. You are like the servant. You must forgive from your heart before your heavenly Father will forgive you."

1. *How many times did Jesus tell Peter to forgive a person?*
2. *What did this parable mean?*

Mary and Martha

Luke 10:38-42

While Jesus was teaching, he often went to the city of Bethany to visit with the family of Martha, her sister Mary, and their brother Lazarus. Mary had once anointed Jesus' feet and wiped them with her hair. She enjoyed sitting at Jesus' feet listening to him talk. These three were friends of Jesus.

Martha was busy working in the house. She finally came in and said to Jesus, "Jesus, do you not care that my sister has left me all of the work to do? Doesn't that bother you?"

"Martha," Jesus said, "do not be troubled by so many things. Mary has chosen to love me, and that cannot be taken from her."

1. *Who were Mary, Martha and Lazarus?*
2. *Why was Martha upset with her sister?*

"Come To Me, Little Children"

Matthew 19:13-15 and Mark 10:13-16

One day Jesus was teaching when a group of mothers came forth with their little children. They asked Jesus to touch them and pray for them.

The disciples tried to push the mothers and children away. They thought Jesus was too busy to be bothered with small children. "The master has important work to do," they said.

About that time Jesus saw the mothers and their children. He called to the children. Jesus felt sorry for the disciples. "Never forbid little children to come to me, for such is the kingdom of God. You must receive the kingdom of God like a little child to enter into it." He took the children in his arms and gave them love.

Jesus knew that the innocent children would easily believe him. They could also lead the older people to him. He knew their hearts were tender.

1. *Why did the mothers bring the children to Jesus?*
2. *What did Jesus tell the disciples about the children?*

Seventy New Disciples

Luke 10:1-24

Jesus knew his days on earth were short. He wanted more people to hear the gospel, so he decided to chose seventy other men who had followed him and knew his word. He gave them power to heal the sick. He sent them out, two at a time, to preach in the cities.

Before they left, he gave the seventy the same rules that he had given the twelve disciples.

He told them, "I send you out as lambs among wolves. Do not take money or food. Take only the shoes you wear. Go straight to the towns to heal the sick and preach to the people. The kingdom of God is coming."

When their mission was over, they returned to tell Jesus about the good things that had happened. They rejoiced because they healed the sick and taught many.

Jesus turned to his disciples and told them, "Blessed are those that see these things. Many prophets and kings wanted to see what you see, but they did not."

Jesus, too, rejoiced that his followers had preached the good news far and wide.

1. *Who did Jesus send out to preach?*
2. *What did the men take with them?*

The Good Samaritan

Luke 10:25-37

Once Jesus was teaching some lawyers. One said, "Teacher, what must I do to have eternal life?" "What is written in the law," Jesus replied.

The man answered: "Love the Lord your God with all your heart and with all your soul and with all your strength and with all of your mind. Love your neighbor as yourself."

But then he asked Jesus, "But who is my neighbor?"

Jesus explained with this story. A man was going from Jerusalem to Jericho when he was attacked by robbers. They took his clothes, beat him, and left him almost dead. A priest came down the same road. When he saw the man, he passed on the opposite side. A Levite came by. He, too, passed on the other side. But a Samaritan saw the man and took pity on him. He bandaged his wounds. Then he put the man on his own donkey, took him to an inn, and took care of him.

The next day he gave the innkeeper two silver coins. He told the innkeeper to look after him. He promised to pay for any additional costs.

"Which of these three do you think was a neighbor to the man who was robbed?" said Jesus.

The lawyer replied, "The one who had mercy on him." Jesus told him to go and do likewise.

1. *Who didn't help the wounded Samaritan?*
2. *Who is a friend and neighbor?*

Lazarus Is Raised from the Dead

John 11:1-54

Lazarus, the brother of Mary and Martha from Bethany, was very sick. This was the same Mary who cleaned Jesus' feet with her hair. The sisters sent word to Jesus that their brother was close to death.

He waited two more days before he returned to Judea. The disciples were worried about Jesus returning to Judea because when he was last there, people tried to stone and kill him. They did not want him to go back.

Jesus answered, "Our friend Lazarus has fallen asleep; but I am going there to wake him." The disciples thought sleep would make him better. But Jesus was talking about death. "Lazarus is dead. I am glad I was not there, for now you will believe."

When Jesus arrived, Lazarus had already been in the tomb for four days. Many had come to comfort Martha and Mary. Martha met Jesus with anger, "If you had been here, my brother would not have died. Jesus told her, "Your brother will rise again."

Martha replied, "I know he will rise on the final resurrection day."

Jesus answered, "I am the resurrection and the life. He who believes in me will live, even though he dies, and whoever lives and believes in me will never die." "I believe you are truly the Christ," said Martha.

Martha went home and told Mary to go see Jesus. When Mary reached the place where Jesus was, she fell at his feet and said, "Lord, if you had been here, my brother would not have died."

"Where have you laid him?" he asked. Mary and Martha led Jesus to the tomb. "Take away the stone," he said.

"Lord, by this time there will be a bad smell," said Martha. Jesus answered, "You must believe, Martha, to see the glory of God."

They took away the stone. Jesus called in a loud voice, "Lazarus, come out!" The dead man came out with his hands and feet still wrapped with strips of linen

Some Jews who had visited with Mary told the Pharisees what Jesus had done. A meeting was called of the Sanhedrin, the governing body.

It was the high priest Caiaphas who said, "It is better for us that one man should die for the people than that our whole nation should be destroyed. Let us put this man to death." A plan was made to take his life.

Jesus could no longer move about publicly among the Jews. He stayed close to his disciples.

1. *What happened to Lazarus? What did Jesus do for Lazarus?*
2. *Why were the rulers worried?*

The Lost Sheep

Luke 15:1-10

The tax collectors and "sinners" all gathered around to listen to Jesus. It was the Pharisees who muttered, "This man welcomes sinners. He even eats with them."

Then Jesus told them this parable. Suppose one of you has a hundred sheep and loses one of them. You would leave the ninety-nine to hunt for the one. After finding it, you would joyfully take it home. Then you would probably call friends and neighbors and say, "Rejoice with me, I have found my lost sheep." I can be honest, there will be more rejoicing in Heaven over one sinner who repents than over ninety-nine righteous persons.

1. *What did the Pharisees say about the people who spent time with Jesus?*
2. *What was the parable Jesus told?*

The Parable of the Prodigal Son

Luke 15:11-32

Jesus told the listeners this story. There was a man who had two sons. The younger one said, "Father, I want my share of the money that I am to have when you die." The father divided his wealth between his two sons. The younger one packed his belongings and went on a long trip. He spent his money generously. Actually, he wasted most of it having a good time, spending it on friends.

About this time there was a famine. The young man became hungry. He tried to work for a farmer tending hogs. He was so hungry, he would have eaten the food for the hogs.

He was so miserable. He remembered that his father's servants always had plenty to eat. He decided to return to his father's home and tell him how he had sinned. Maybe he could be a servant for his father.

One day his father saw a man coming up the road who was ragged. When the young man got closer, the father realized it was his son. He ran to him and threw his arms around him.

"Father, I have sinned." Before he said more his father ordered a robe for him. He put a ring on his finger and shoes on his feet. He had a feast prepared. "My son who was lost is now found."

The older son had been working in the field. He heard the commotion and returned to see what was happening.

The servants told him his brother had returned. The older brother was not happy. "I have served you faithfully all these years, but you do not rejoice over me. My brother spent all of his money. Now when he returns, you celebrate."

The father saw the jealousy of the older son. "You have always been with me. Everything I have is yours. But I must rejoice at my son's return. He was lost, but now he is found."

Jesus showed that he came to help those who were sinful and greedy.

1. *What did the younger son want from the father?*
2. *What was the lesson Jesus was teaching in this parable?*

The Unjust Judge

Luke 18:1-14

God does not always answer prayer right away. This story is to encourage people to pray and to continue praying.

A poor woman had been wronged by an enemy. She went to the city judge for help.

The judge was not fair or good. He was not interested in helping the widow. She said, "You must be fair in this matter." She returned time after time trying to get help from the judge.

Finally the judge decided to help her because she was such a bother. "I will do what this widow wants so she will leave me alone," he said.

Then Jesus said, "Learn a lesson from this judge. Don't you think God will be fair when you pray? Will He wait? He will act quickly. I hope I will find faith on this earth when I return."

1. *Why did the judge help the woman?*
2. *What does Jesus want to find when he returns?*

Saved by Faith

Luke 18:35-43

As Jesus arrived in Jericho, a blind man was sitting by the roadside begging. He heard the noise as Jesus approached. He asked what was happening. He was told that Jesus of Nazareth was passing by.

He yelled out, "Jesus, Son of David, have mercy on me!"

Those who were leading the way scolded him. They told him to be quiet. But he shouted even louder, "Jesus, Son of David, have mercy on me!"

Jesus stopped. He asked that the man be brought to him. When the man came near, Jesus asked, "What is it you want from me?"

"Oh, Lord, I want to see," he replied.

Jesus said to him, You now have sight. Your faith has healed you. He immediately received his sight. He stood up and followed Jesus, praising God. All of the people who saw this also praised God.

1. *Why did the followers try to stop the blind man from talking to Jesus?*
2. *Why was his sight restored?*

Zaccheus in the Tree

Luke 19:1-10

Zaccheus, a rich man, was the head tax collector in Jericho. He heard that Jesus was going to pass through town. He wanted to see Jesus, but he was extremely short. So he ran ahead of the crowd and climbed a sycamore tree.

When Jesus reached the tree, he looked up and said to him, "Zaccheus, come down from that tree immediately. I want to stay at your house today." Quickly Zaccheus climbed down from the tree. He welcomed Jesus.

All of the people saw this and began to mutter. "He is going to be the guest of a 'sinner'!"

Zaccheus looked up at Jesus, "Look, Lord, I will give half of my possessions to the poor. If I have cheated anyone, I will pay back four times the amount."

Jesus said to him, "Today salvation has come to this house. Remember, the Son of Man came to save what was lost."

1. *Why did Zaccheus climb the tree?*
2. *Why did Jesus decide to go to the home of Zaccheus?*

Palm Sunday

Matthew 21:1-11; Mark 11:1-11;
Luke 19:29-40; John 12: 12-19

Everyone in Jerusalem was excited. Many had come to Jerusalem for Passover. Many wanted to meet the Jesus they had heard so much about.

As Jesus and the disciples arrived near Jerusalem, Jesus told two of them to go to the nearby town to get a donkey and a colt which had never been ridden. "Tell them the Lord has need of it."

The disciples brought the colt to Jesus. They put their coats on its back. As they walked along the road, many people spread their coats on the ground in front of Jesus. Some waved palm branches. The whole crowd joyfully praised God for the miracles they had seen.

Blessed is the king who comes in the name
  of the Lord!
Peace in Heaven and glory in the highest!

Some of the Pharisees said, "Teacher, stop your disciples!" He answered, "If they were silent, the stones would shout."

Jesus rode up Mount Moriah to the temple while the people shouted, "Hosanna to the Son of David!" "Here is Jesus, the prophet from Nazareth of Galilee."

1. *How did the people greet Jesus?*
2. *What did Jesus say would happen if the people were silent?*

Jesus Will Return

Matthew 25:31-46

Jesus told his disciples that when the time came for the end of the world the Son of Man would come in his glory. I will sit upon his throne. All of the nations of the world will gather there. I will divide good from evil. Those who believe in me will be on his right. Those who are bad will be on my left. The good and evil will be divided like the shepherd divides the sheep from the goats.

To those on the right I will say, "You are blessed by our Father. I was hungry and you gave me food. I was thirsty, and you gave me something to drink. When I was a stranger, you welcomed me. I was naked and you gave me clothes. You visited me in prison."

And one said, "Lord, when did we do all of this for you?"

He answered, "Whenever you helped one needy person, you helped me."

"I will tell those on my left to go away. Go to the devil and his eternal fire. You never did any good things for me or any part of my family. When you refuse to help anyone, you refuse to help me."

Jesus then told the disciples: "The Passover will come in two days. Then I will be arrested and crucified."

1. *What happens when you help the people around you?*
2. *How did Jesus divide people for the end of time?*

The Last Supper

Matthew 26:17-30; Mark 14:12-26;
Luke 22:3-39; John 13

The disciples asked, "Where should we make preparations to eat the Passover?" Jesus told them to go into the city and find a certain man. They were to tell him that Jesus and the disciples would be celebrating the Passover at his house.

When they found the man, he led them upstairs to a guest room. That evening Jesus and the other ten joined Peter and John. Jesus told them this would be his last supper with them. Sadness fell over the room.

The table was set with the supper. Jesus took the bread and gave thanks. He broke it into pieces for each of the twelve. "Take, eat. This is my body. Do this in remembrance of me. Then he took a cup of wine and passed it to each one while saying, "This is my blood, shed for you so your sins may be taken away. Drink this in remembrance of me."

The disciples could not believe he would be taken from them. As they ate, they wondered who would be the greatest in Jesus' kingdom.

Jesus knew what they were thinking. He got up from the table and tied a towel around his waist. He filled a basin with water and began to wash their feet. The disciples were so surprised. Why was Jesus doing this? Peter said, "Lord, you will never wash my feet!" "If I do not wash your feet, then you will not have a part in my kingdom," said Jesus.

Peter quickly answered, "Then wash my feet, hands and head!"

Jesus said, "I have washed your feet, so you should go and wash the feet of others. This is an example for you. You should do to each other as I have done to you. The servant is not greater than the master."

Jesus looked around and said, "One of you will betray me." The disciples were shocked. Most asked, "Lord, is it I?"

Jesus said, "It is the one who receives this piece of bread." Jesus gave the bread to Judas Iscariot. Immediately Judas left the room. The disciples were confused.

Jesus told the disciples they should not be afraid. "I will rise again."

Peter said, "Lord, I will never leave you!" But Jesus answered him, "Peter, before the rooster crows again, you will deny me three times."

The men sang a hymn together before they left the upper room and went to the Garden of Gethsemane.

1. *What food and drink was at the Last Supper? What did it represent?*
2. *What did Jesus do for the disciples? Why?*

The Garden of Gethsemane

Matthew 26:30-46

Jesus, Peter, James and John went to the Mount of Olives to a garden called Gethsemane. Jesus told the disciples to sit while he went away to pray. He said, "I am so overwhelmed with sorrow. Please stay here and keep watch with me."

He went a little farther then fell on his face on the ground. He prayed, "Father, I really do not want to do this. Yet if this is what you want, then I will do as you ask."

He returned to the disciples and found them asleep. "Can you not keep watch for one hour?"

He went away a second time. This time he said, "Father, may your will be done."

He returned and found them asleep again. He went away and prayed a third time, saying the same thing.

He returned to the disciples and said, "The hour is near. The Son of Man is betrayed into the hands of sinners. Rise, and let us go!"

1. *What did the disciples do while Jesus was praying?*
2. *What did Jesus discuss with his Father?*

Jesus Is Arrested

Matthew 26:14-16; 47-56
Luke 22:3-6; 47-53

The chief priests and teachers of law were now trying to find a way to get rid of Jesus. They were afraid of the reaction that the people would have if Jesus was put to death.

Judas Iscariot, one of the twelve disciples, went to the chief priests and the officers of the temple guard. He discussed with them how he might betray Jesus. "What will you give me if I hand him over to you?" They were delighted he came to them, so they agreed to give him money. They gave him 30 pieces of silver. From then on Judas watched for an opportunity to betray Jesus.

While Jesus was speaking, Judas came up with a large crowd. Many in the crowd, sent by the chief priests and elders, carried swords and clubs.

Judas the betrayer had arranged for a signal: "Arrest the man I kiss." Judas walked up to Jesus who said, "Friend, do what you came for."

Several men stepped forward to arrest Jesus. One who was with Jesus reached out and struck the servant of a high priest, cutting off his ear.

"Draw back your sword," Jesus said, "for all who draw the sword will die by the sword." He then looked at Judas, "Why do you come with swords and clubs to arrest me? Do you think I am a thief? Every day you see me in the temple. What the prophets have written is happening."

All of the disciples ran from the garden.

1. *How could the crowd tell who Jesus was?*
2. *What did the disciples do?*

Peter's Denial

Matthew 26:69-75; Mark 14:66-72;
Luke 22:52-62; John 18:16-18, 25-27

While Jesus was being questioned, Peter stood in the courtyard of the high priest. It was a cold evening. There was a fire in the middle of the courtyard. Peter stood by the fire seeking warmth.

A servant girl of the high priest came by. She stopped when she saw Peter. She looked at him closely. "Weren't you with that Jesus of ·Nazareth?" But he denied it. "I don't know what you are talking about." He walked quickly to the entryway.

There another girl looked at him and told the crowd of people, "This fellow is one of them. He was with that Jesus." Again Peter denied it.

After a little while, others standing close by said, "You must be one of the followers for you are a Galilean."

Peter yelled at the crowd, "I don't know the man you are talking about!"

Immediately Peter heard a rooster crow. Sadly, he remembered the words Jesus spoke to him: "Before the rooster crows, you will deny me three times." He went outside and cried.

1. *How many times did Peter deny Jesus?*
2. *Why did he cry?*

The Death of Judas Iscariot

Matthew 27:1-10

Judas Iscariot, the man who betrayed Jesus, thought Jesus would not die. Perhaps he thought a man who performed miracles on others would save himself. But the men who were guarding Jesus had beat him and mocked him. Judas saw that Jesus was bound and beaten. He heard the rulers discussing putting Jesus to death.

He returned the thirty pieces of silver to the chief priests and elders. "I have betrayed an innocent man." They replied, "Why do we care! That is your responsibility!"

Judas threw the money in the temple and left. He went away and hanged himself.

The chief priests could not put blood money in the treasury. They decided to use the money to buy a potter's field, a burial place for foreigners and poor people. It is called the Field of Blood.

1. *Did Judas believe Jesus would die? Why not?*
2. *What did the chief priests do with the "blood money"?*

Jesus Appears before Pilate and Herod

Luke 22:66-23:25; Matthew 26:63-66;
Mark 14:61-63; John 18:19-21

Jesus was led before the council of the elders at daybreak. "If you are the Christ tell us," they said.

Jesus answered, "You will not believe me. But from now on, the Son of Man will be seated at the right hand of God."

The whole council rose and led him to Pilate. "This man is an evil-doer." Pilate listened to the council. "Are you the king of the Jews?" Jesus answered, "It is as you say."

Then Pilate announced to the chief priests, "I see no reason to charge this man with a crime." But they cried out, "He agitates people from here to Galilee." Pilate said, "If this man is from Galilee, he needs to go before the ruler, Herod."

Herod was pleased to have a chance to see Jesus. He had heard so much about him. Perhaps he would perform a miracle for Herod's court.

He asked many questions, but Jesus gave no answers. Everyone in the room, including the priests and lawyers, were making fun of him.

Herod also mocked him. He let his soldiers dress him in an elegant robe. He then sent him back to Pilate.

Pilate called those concerned and told them that neither he nor Herod could find charges against Jesus. "I will punish him and then release him. You know it is the custom to set a prisoner free during Passover."

At that time there was a prisoner named Barabbas who was a robber and a murderer.

The rulers talked to the crowd. They told the crowd to ask for Barabbas.

Pilate said, "Who shall it be? Do you want Jesus, King of the Jews, or do you want Barabbas?" The crowd yelled, "Give us Barabbas!" Pilate asked them again. They shouted, "Crucify him! Crucify him!"

Finally Pilate granted their demand. He released Barabbas. He knew Jesus was a good and fair man, but he sent him to the cross.

1. Why did Pilate want to free Jesus?
2. What did the people demand of Pilate?

On the Cross

Matthew 27:33-44; Mark 15:22-32;
Luke 23:26-43; John 19:17-24

Jesus was too weak to carry his own cross. As they were leaving the city, they met a man named Simon of Cyrene. He was forced to carry the cross. They stopped at a place called Golgotha in Hebrew, the Jewish language, or Calvary in Latin (both mean the Place of the Skull).

They offered Jesus a drink which would dull his senses and make the pain easier, but he wanted to have a clear mind. He knew he would suffer.

They laid the cross on the ground. Jesus was stretched across it. They drove nails in his hands and feet to fasten him to the cross. Then they stood the cross upright and stuck it in the ground. While they were doing this Jesus said, "Father, forgive them for they don't know what they are doing." While watching over him, the soldiers cast lots for his clothes.

Pilate had a sign placed above his head which read:

THIS IS JESUS
KING OF THE JEWS.

It was written in three languages, Hebrew, Latin and Greek.

There were two robbers who were crucified with him, one on his right and one on his left. Most who walked by yelled insults at him. "If you are the Son of God, come down from the cross!" "He saved others, but he can't save himself!"

1. *Who carried the cross for Jesus? Why?*
2. *What did Pilate have written on the sign above Jesus' head?*

The Death of Jesus

Matthew 27:45-56; Mark 15:33-41
Luke 23:44-49; John 19:28-30

By the cross of Jesus stood his mother, filled with sadness for her son. With her was John, the disciple Jesus loved best. Others present were Mary wife of Cleopas, his mother's sister; and a woman named Mary Magdalene.

It was now about the sixth hour. The whole world was dark because the sun was not shining. Jesus was in great pain. He cried out, "My God, why have you forsaken me!" Later he said, "I thirst." Someone dipped a sponge in vinegar, put it on a reed, and gave it to him to drink.

Then Jesus spoke his last words. He called out in a loud voice, "Father into your hands I commit my spirit." After saying this, he died. At that moment the curtain in the temple split in two.

The centurion walked up to the cross and praised God. "Truly, he is the Son of God."

1. *What were some statements Jesus made while on the cross?*
2. *What happened to the earth when Jesus died?*

At the Tomb

Matthew 27:57-66; Luke 23:50-56; John 19:38-42

After Jesus died one of the soldiers ran a spear into his side to make certain he was truly dead. Water and blood ran out of the wound.

It was Joseph of Arimathea who asked Pilate for the body of Jesus. He was a follower and a good man, but had told few people because of his fears of the Jewish leaders.

Joseph took Jesus' body off of the cross. Nicodemus, the man who had come to Jesus in the night, was also present. He brought myrrh and aloes. The two covered the body with spices and wrapped it in linen, then placed it in a tomb that Joseph had cut out of the rock. He rolled a big stone in front of the tomb and left the garden.

Mary Magdalene and Mary sat in the garden by the tomb.

The next day some of the rulers went to Pilate to remind him that Jesus had said he would rise again in three days. Pilate put a guard on the tomb so the disciples could not enter.

1. *Who did Pilate give permission to take the body of Jesus?*
2. *Why was a guard placed at the tomb?*

The Resurrection

Matthew 28:1-10; Mark 16:1-8; Luke 24:1-10

The Sun was rising. It was Sunday morning, three days since Jesus had died. Mary Magdalene and the other Mary went back to look at the tomb.

Just then there was a powerful earthquake. An angel came down from Heaven, rolled back the stone, and sat on it. Jesus stepped out in clothes as white as snow. The guards shook with fear.

The angel spoke to the women. "Do not be afraid. Jesus is not here. He has risen, just as he said he would. Come here and see where he was, then go tell the disciples. He is on his way to Galilee. Go there to see him."

The women ran quickly from the tomb, afraid yet happy. Suddenly Jesus met them. "Hello," he said. They fell at his feet and worshiped him. "Don't be afraid. Go tell everyone to come to Galilee."

1. *Who rolled back the rock on the tomb?*
2. *What did Jesus tell the women to do?*

On the Road to Emmaus

Luke 24:13-27

On that same day two of them were going to Emmaus, about seven miles from Jerusalem. They were discussing everything that happened when Jesus started walking with them, but they did not recognize him.

"What are you talking about?" Jesus asked. "Have you not heard what has been happening in Jerusalem?" one questioned. "What is that?" he asked.

"About the prophet, Jesus of Nazareth. The chief priests and rulers let him be sentenced to death. He was crucified. Some of our women went to the tomb today and found it empty. They even saw visions of angels who told them he was alive. Some of his disciples went to the tomb later, but did not see him."

"How foolish you are! Don't you remember all of the scriptures as you learned it." Even though they still had not recognized him, they asked him to stay with them. When he sat with them at the table, he took bread and gave thanks. Immediately they recognized him, but he disappeared.

They returned to Jerusalem immediately to tell the other disciples what they saw.

1. *Who walked with the two to Emmaus?*
2. *When did they realize it was Jesus?*

.

Jesus in Jerusalem

Luke 24:38-49; John 20:24-28

The disciples were in Jerusalem discussing the recent events. Jesus appeared to them. "Why are you doubting all of the events?" he asked, "Look at my hands and feet. Touch me. I am not a ghost. A ghost does not have flesh and bones."

Thomas, one of the disciples, was not present when Jesus first appeared. When the disciples told him what had happened, he said, "Unless I see the nail marks and put my hand on his side, I will not believe it."

A week later Jesus stood among them and said, "Peace be with you! Thomas, touch my side, look at my hands. Stop doubting and believe!"

Jesus said, "Because you have seen me, you believe. Blessed are those who have not seen me and yet still believe."

1. *How did Jesus prove he was not a ghost?*
2. *Why did Thomas doubt that Jesus had returned?*

Peter's Love

John 21:1-27

Some of the disciples, including Peter, decided to go fishing in the Sea of Tiberias. They fished all night but did not catch anything. At daybreak, Jesus stood on the beach. The disciples did not recognize him.

"Did you catch anything?" he asked. "No," they replied. "Throw your net on the right side of the boat." Immediately the net was full of fish.

John told Peter, "It is the Lord." Peter was so excited he fell in the water. While the others rowed ashore, Peter swam. There on the beach was a fire with fish and bread. "Come have breakfast," Jesus said.

After breakfast Jesus asked Peter, "Do you love me more than these fish?"

"Of course, Lord, you know that I love you."

"Then feed my lambs."

Jesus asked the question a second time, "Peter, do you love me?"

"Yes, Lord. I love you."

"Then tend my sheep."

Then for a third time, Jesus asked, "Do you love me?" Peter was hurt that Jesus continued to ask this question. "Lord, you know that I love you."

"I will tell you, Peter, someone else will take you where you don't want to go." Someday Peter would die serving God.

1. *What happened when the disciples caught no fish?*
2. *Why was Peter hurt Jesus kept asking the same question?*

The Ascension

Matthew 28:16-20

The followers met on a mountain in Galilee. Jesus appeared to more than 500 people. "I will have all power in Heaven. When the Holy Spirit comes to you, you shall have new power. Go all over the world and speak my name. Baptize in the name of the Father, and of the Son, and of the Holy Spirit. Teach the commandments that you have learned. I will be with you, even to the end of the earth."

Jesus was seen eight times after he rose from the dead. He stayed with the disciples for forty days talking about God's kingdom.

Later Jesus led the disciples to the Mount of Olives. He lifted his hands and blessed them. As he did he started to rise from the earth. Soon he was above the clouds.

While they were looking toward Heaven, they saw angels. "Jesus will come again to earth, as it has been said." The disciples were glad.

They spent their time in the temple praising God.

1. *What did Jesus tell the disciples to do?*
2. *What does the word ascension mean?*

Pentecost

Acts 2:14-47

With Judas no longer a part of the group, the disciples decided to pray about adding a twelfth member. After praying, and casting lots, it was decided that Mathias would be asked to be the twelfth. From this time on the disciples were called apostles, "the men sent forth."

Peter then preached to a large number of followers. "Everyone listen to me, all of the prophets' words have come to pass. This is the day when everyone who shall call on the Lord shall be saved. Jesus of Nazareth was put on the cross by evil men, but God has raised him from death. We have seen him and know him to be the Lord and the Christ."

Many people understood his words and starting believing. Peter told them to turn from sin and be baptized.

That day over 3,000 were baptized by the apostles and joined the Church of Christ. They met in the upper room, worshiped in the temple, and listened to the teachings of the apostles.

And every day more and more were uniting with the Church.

1. *What does apostle mean?*
2. *What did Peter tell those gathered?*

Peter Heals the Beggar

Acts 3:1-10

Peter and John were going to the temple to pray. There was a man who was crippled who was taken to the temple gate (called Beautiful) each day to beg from those going into the temple. When he saw Peter and John, he asked them for money.

Peter looked straight at the man and said, "Look at us! We don't have silver or gold, but we do have something we can give you. In the name of Jesus of Nazareth, walk!"

Peter took his hand and helped him up. Even though this man had been crippled since birth, he stood up and began to walk. When people saw him walking, they recognized him. They were amazed at what had happened to him. The beggar went into the temple with Peter and John. He was walking, leaping and praising God.

1. *What did Peter have to give the beggar?*
2. *What did the man do as he went into the temple?*

Peter Talks with the People

Acts 3:11-26

The beggar held on to Peter and John as he entered the temple. The people continued to watch in amazement. When Peter saw their surprise he said, "People of Israel, why are you so shocked? Why do you stare at us as if we made him walk? God of Abraham and our fathers glorified Jesus. You turned him over to Pilate to be killed. You chose Barabbas the murderer instead. You disowned the Holy One. But God raised him from the dead, for we witnessed it. Faith in the name of Jesus Christ has made this man strong.

"I know you did not realize what you were doing. But now you must believe in God to have your sins removed. In time, God will send Jesus to us again."

Peter and John talked to the people. The priests were irritated that the disciples were teaching in the temple. They arrested both men. They were held until the next day. But 5,000 people became followers of Jesus that day.

1. *What made the beggar strong?*
2. *Why were the priests irritated with Peter and John?*

The Apostles Are Persecuted

Acts 5:12-42

Although they were told not to, Peter and John continued to preach. They performed more miracles. Sick were brought to them. Crowds gathered in Jerusalem. People asked for forgiveness of sins.

The high priest and the members of the Sadducees were very jealous. They arrested the apostles and put them in jail again.

During the night an angel of the Lord opened the doors of the jail and let them out. "Go stand in the temple courts and tell the people the message of new life."

At daybreak they entered the temple courts as they were told. They preached to all who were there.

When the high priests and his men arrived, they called a meeting of the Sanhedrin. They sent officers to the jail for the disciples. But when the officers arrived, the men were not there. The officers reported to the Sanhedrin that the doors were securely locked, but no one was inside. Everyone was puzzled.

Someone came to report the apostles were again preaching and teaching in the temple. The officers went to the temple to get the men. They did not use force because they were afraid the people would stone them.

The apostles stood before the Sanhedrin to be questioned. "Didn't we instruct you not to preach your word again? You are trying to make us feel guilty for killing that man."

Peter and the other apostles replied, "We must obey God instead of men! God raised Jesus from the dead. You had him hanged on a cross. We are witness to these things and so is the Holy Spirit."

The Sanhedrin considered putting the apostles to death. They were furious with them. But a teacher named Gamaliel advised, "Think carefully about this matter. If they come from God, you can't stop them."

The apostles were whipped and ordered not to speak in Jesus' name again. The apostles left the Sanhedrin and felt happy because they were worthy of suffering for Jesus. They continued to preach the good news brought by Jesus Christ.

1. *What did the disciples do when the angels released them from prison?*
2. *What was the warning given by the teacher Gamaliel?*

A Man with Faith

Acts 6:1-15

The number of disciples was also increasing. Even priests were turning to Christ.

Seven new men were chosen from the followers. It was their job to care for the sharing of food among the believers. The word of God spread.

One of the chosen was Stephen, a man full of faith. He did miraculous things among the people. Some of the Jews argued with Stephen. They couldn't stand up against his wisdom, so they secretly paid people to say terrible things about him. "We've heard Stephen say things against Moses and God." "We have heard him say Jesus of Nazareth will destroy this place."

Stephen was forced to go to the council of rulers. People lied about him there. People said he wanted to change traditions that Moses gave.

The high priest looked at Stephen. "Is what they are saying true?" Everyone present looked into the face of Stephen. What they saw wa a face like an angel.

1. *What kind of man was Stephen?*
2. *What were some of the lies told about him?*

Saul

Acts 9:1-31

There was a young man named Saul who supported the death of Stephen. When he ran into believers outside of Jerusalem, he yelled threats at them. He was responsible for some disciples being jailed.

Saul asked the high priest for permission to go to Damascus. He would arrest anyone on his way who followed Jesus. As Saul entered Damascus a light from heaven flashed around him. He fell to the ground. A voice said, "Saul, why are you defying me?" Saul said, "Who are you?" The answer was, "I am Jesus, the one you are harassing."

Saul was blinded by the light from heaven. He continued to listen to Jesus. "Get up and go into the city. There you will be told what to do."

The men with Saul were speechless. Saul got up, but he could not see. He was blind. His men led him into Damascus. For three days he could not see. He did not eat or drink anything.

In Damascus there was a disciple named Ananias. The Lord came to him and told him to go to Straight Street and ask for a man from Tarsus named Saul. "He has seen you in a vision. You are to place your hands on him to restore his sight."

"Lord I have heard reports that this man is harmful. He has come with authority from the chief priests to arrest all who preach in your name."

But the Lord told Ananias that he would make Saul an instrument of his name before the Gentiles and their kings.

As he was told, Ananias went to the house. He placed his hands on Saul and said, "It was the Lord Jesus who appeared on the road to you. He has sent me to restore your sight so you will be filled with the Holy Spirit." Immediately Saul could see again. He got up and was baptized. He then ate some food to restore his strength.

Saul stayed in Damascus for several days. Immediately he began to preach in the synagogues about Jesus. All who heard him were astonished.

The Jews became fearful of his powerful preaching. They plotted to kill him, but Saul learned of their plan.

They had guards on the city gate, but Saul's followers took him at night and lowered him in a basket through an opening in the wall.

He returned to Jerusalem and tried to join the disciples. They were all afraid of him. Finally Barnabas took him to the apostles. Saul stayed with them. When he tried to continue preaching, the Jews tried to kill him again. Finally he was taken to Caesarea and sent to Tarsus.

For a while the whole church had peace and continued to grow.

1. *Why did Saul go to Damascus?*
2. *What did Ananias do for Saul?*

Peter's Vision

Acts 10:1-48

At Caesarea there was man named Cornelius. He was a centurion. He and all of his family were devout and God-fearing and gave generously to the poor.

One day Cornelius had a vision from an angel of God. "Your prayers and gifts are a memorial to God. Send to Joppa for a man named Peter." That day Cornelius sent one of his servants for Peter.

Peter was staying in the home of Simon the tanner. He went to the roof to pray. While there he had a vision. God told him to kill and eat. Peter did not understand. He had never eaten anything unclean. But the voice spoke to him three times. God told him that anything that God made was clean.

Peter was curious about the vision. The men sent by Cornelius arrived and called for Peter. Peter was also given a sign by God to go with these men.

The next day Peter left with the them. As Peter entered the house, Cornelius fell at his feet. Peter told him to get up. "I am only a man."

Peter went outside and found a large gathering of people He knew it was unlawful for a Jew to associate with a Gentile. Peter now understood his vision. He should call no man unpure or unclean. He asked why he was needed.

Cornelius said, "Four days ago a man came to my house. He had on bright clothes. He told me to send for you, and you are kind enough to come. All here are in the presence of God to listen to you."

Peter told them the good news about Jesus Christ. He talked about forgiveness of sins. He knew the Father's gift of the Holy Spirit had fallen on the Gentiles. Peter said, "Can anyone keep these people from being baptized?" All were baptized in the name of Jesus Christ. They invited Peter to stay with them for a few days.

1. *Who came to Cornelius?*
2. *Why did Peter know he should be with the Gentiles?*

The Christians of Antioch

Acts 11:19-30

Many of the followers had been scattered when Stephen was persecuted. Some went to Antioch to preach the good news. The Lord was with them. Many people turned to the Lord as they preached.

News of this reached the church in Jerusalem, so Barnabas was sent to encourage them and preach. He was a good man, full of the Holy Spirit.

After preaching a while Barnabas went to Tarsus to look for Saul. When he found him, he brought him back to Antioch. For a whole year Barnabas and Saul met with the church and taught a large number of people It was first at Antioch that the disciples were called Christians.

At that time there was a famine. Many believers in Judea were without food. The church in Antioch sent Barnabas and Saul to give aid to the churches in Judea.

1. *What kind of man was Barnabas?*
2. *What was the name given the believers in Antioch?*

The Return to Antioch

Acts 14: 27:15:1-21

By now Saul had traveled and preached for some time. He was now called Paul. It was time to return to Antioch once again.

On arriving there, they called the people of the church together. Paul announced that through God he had opened the church to the Gentiles.

But then people came to Antioch from Judea. "The Gentiles must keep the law of Moses to be saved." Paul and Barnabas had a sharp debate with this group. Paul and Barnabas were appointed to go to Jerusalem to discuss this question with the apostles and elders.

They were welcomed in Jerusalem. They reported everything God had done through them in all of their travels.

The question then came up. Some of the Pharisees stood up and said, "The Gentiles must be circumcised and required to obey the law of Moses."

After much discussion, Peter addressed them: "Friends, you know that God let the Gentiles hear from my lips the message of the gospel. God showed that he accepted them. He made no distinction between us and them. He purified their hearts by faith. We believe it is through the grace of our Lord Jesus that we are saved, just as they are."

The room was silent as they listened to Barnabas and Paul tell about the miracles and wonders God had done among the Gentiles. Then James said, "It is my opinion that we should not make it difficult for the Gentiles who are turning to God. We should write to them and tell them how to live in God's grace."

1. *What did the people of Judea want the Gentiles to do?*
2. *How did Peter say people are saved?*

The Death of the Apostle Paul

Acts 28:30; 2 Timothy 4:6-8

Paul preached for many years. His journeys took him far and wide. He started churches and drew many faithful to God. Not everyone agreed with Paul's teachings. Often he was ridiculed. Once Paul was on a ship that broke apart in a storm. He survived and lived on an island named Malta. Paul also lived in Rome for a while.

He had many accusers who told lies about him. Others questioned what he taught. Paul's accusers never came from Jerusalem to blame him in Rome. He waited two years. Paul loved and cared for all of the churches he had started.

Paul continued to travel. He visited Timothy in Ephesus. It was during this time that Rome burned. It is thought that he might have been in Spain at this time. But Christians had been blamed for the burning. This may be why Paul was arrested. God decided he would not be saved this time. Instead, the apostle was convicted and beheaded by the Romans.

Before he died, Paul wrote Timothy: "The time has come for my departure. I have fought the good fight, I have finished the race, I have kept the faith. The Lord has a crown awaiting me. He will give it to me the day he returns. All of those who love him will receive a crown."

1. What did Paul think about the churches he started?
2. What did Paul write to Timothy before he died?